WILLIAM
SHAKESPEARE'S
BREXIT

WILLIAM
SHAKESPEARE'S

BREXIT

A POLITICAL SH*TSTORM IN FIVE ACTS

also perform'd under the titles

As EU Like It

- and -

Much Ado About Brexit

BLINK
bringing you closer

Published by Blink Publishing
The Plaza,
535 Kings Road,
Chelsea Harbour,
London, SW10 0SZ

www.blinkpublishing.co.uk

facebook.com/blinkpublishing
twitter.com/blinkpublishing

Hardback – 978-1-78870-254-6
Ebook – 978-1-78870-255-3

A CIP catalogue of this book is available from the British Library.

Front cover illustration by Ella Baron
Printed and bound in Great Britain by Clays Ltd, Elcograf S.p.A

3 5 7 9 10 8 6 4 2

This is a work of fiction. Every reasonable attempt to verify the facts
against available documentation has been made.

Blink Publishing is an imprint of Bonnier Books UK
www.bonnierbooks.co.uk

INTRODUCTION

It's an easy and amusing pastime to imagine how writers of yesteryear would be earning their living today.

Charles Dickens, for example, would probably be chief scriptwriter on *EastEnders*. He was an expert at marshalling a wide and varied array of characters, and his practice of writing in weekly instalments would stand him in good stead for a drumbeat-accompanied cliffhanger every 28 minutes.

Jane Austen would be the godmother of chick-lit. It is, after all, a truth universally acknowledged that pretty much every writer of popular female literature owes an enormous debt to Austen and her original universally-acknowledged truth about single men's fortunes and needs (indeed, Helen Fielding lifted not just the plot of *Pride and Prejudice* but even the name of its antagonist-turned-paramour for *Bridget Jones's Diary*).

William Wordsworth would be carving out a small but lucrative niche writing pithy epigrams for superimposition on heavily-filtered shots of his beloved Lake District (though he might express bemusement at how far the concept of The Cloud has come from his own lonely, wandering version).

And as for the daddy of them all, the Bard himself? Well, he could have turned his hand to pretty much anything and everything, so it's a fair guess that sooner or later he'd have set his sights on Brexit. He would have done so not just because it has proved the defining issue of the age, but also because it has engaged the populace in a manner very rare in politics, and Shakespeare was nothing if not a writer for the people and of the people. If he is seen as elitist at a distance of more than four centuries, he was anything but in his own day.

In terms of popular culture – which is, to use the dominant medium of the day, television – politics since the UK first joined what was then the Common Market in 1973 has been filtered through two series above all. First came *Yes, Minister* (and its sequel, *Yes, Prime Minister*) with its drolly cynical acceptance that the country was really run by the Sir Humphreys of the civil service. In its footsteps, but at some remove, followed *The Thick Of It*, which cast all those in conventional political orbits – cabinet ministers, MPs, civil servants and special advisers – as hapless bystanders to the tyranny of spin and the endless, insatiable news cycle, themselves immortalised in the perpetually enraged figure of Malcolm Tucker.

Shakespeare himself would surely have loved both series, not least for their use of language: Sir Humphrey's pompous circumlocutions designed to pull the wool over the eyes of his supposed masters, and Malcolm's amazingly inventive swearing. Shakespeare's own capacity for insults was impressive: the long litany of abuse which I have Boris Johnson hurling at Michael Gove's voicemail in Act II Scene V are all genuine Shakespearean vituperation.

(To even things up with a Brussels viewpoint, the other fictional character such insults may bring to mind is Tintin's great mate Captain Haddock, whose creator Hergé was of course Belgian. Haddock's repertoire was extensive and often slightly surreal. 'Bashi-bazouk! Lily-livered bandicoots! Addle-pated lumps of anthracite! Macrocephalic baboon! Dictatorial duck-billed diplodocus! Fancy-dress freebooter! Scoffing braggart! Squawking popinjay!' Of these, and many more, Shakespeare himself would have been proud.)

What both *Yes, Minister* and *The Thick Of It* nailed, in their different ways, was the contradictory and often toxic brew at the heart of politics: that even (or especially) those who enter the game with the best of intentions gradually find that very idealism leached out of them, and so any striving for a better world is buried under piles of rubbled feuding and obscured by smokescreens of bitter rivalries.

So too, perhaps, with Brexit. Shakespeare, who understood the dark heart of man's motivations better than almost any other writer in history (though I would also put in an honourable mention for Joseph Conrad here), would have found deep fascination with the figures at the heart of Brexit. Was David Cameron an insouciant fool or a good man undone by the extreme elements of his own party? Was Boris Johnson a true believer in the cause he espoused or a charlatan wedded only to his own advancement? Was Michael Gove a turncoat or a man of principle? Was Theresa May a hopelessly limited operator or the only grown-up in the room? Or were they in some degree all of these at once, and more?

It was initially tempting to try and match these real-life figures with actual Shakespearean characters: Johnson as Falstaff, perhaps; Gove as Iago; May as a cross between a vacillating Hamlet and a Julia Caesar fatally stabbed by her own colleagues. But the events of Brexit are too dramatically rich to be circumscribed by plots dreamed up when the first Queen Elizabeth was on the throne, so in the end it seemed better to let the main characters play themselves, more or less, though some minor characters took on pre-assigned roles (May's advisors Nick Timothy and Fiona Hill as Rosencrantz and Guildenstern, and the Brussels triumvirate of Jean-Claude Juncker, Donald Tusk and Michel Barnier as the three witches who meet on the heath in *Macbeth*).

Shakespeare's plays can be grouped into three main categories: comedy, tragedy and history. Brexit is a little of all three. There were some extremely funny moments during the three years or more which this play covers, and the Brits, whether Leavers or Remainers, consistently proved themselves world class at taking the mickey. Whichever side of the argument you're on, and whether you think Brexit is a triumph or a disaster, the coarsening of political debate and the retreat into entrenched tribalism is surely a tragedy.

As for history: well, as the first country ever to leave the EU we are making history one way or another, though the full impact will take decades to assess. (Nor is where we are now by any means the end of the process. Shakespeare divided one of his histories, *Henry IV*, into two parts, and another, *Henry VI*, into three, and it is entirely possible that in another few years there will be enough material to write *William Shakespeare's Brexit Part II*.)

This play is divided into five acts, just as many of Shakespeare's were. Act I ends with the Referendum being won and lost; Act II covers the subsequent Tory leadership battle and Theresa May's invoking of Article 50; Act III sees her disastrous election campaign of 2017 and equally disastrous party conference speech later in the year; Act IV details her abortive attempts to get her Withdrawal Agreement through Parliament and her subsequent resignation; and Act V comprises the leadership battle which ended with Boris Johnson in Number 10.

I hope you have as much fun reading it as I did writing it.

Boris Starling

August 2019

WILLIAM
SHAKESPEARE'S

BREXIT

A POLITICAL
SH*TSTORM
IN FIVE ACTS

DRAMATIS PERSONAE

LAURA KUENSSBERG, a television journalist

DAVID CAMERON, First of Her Majesty's Ministers

GEORGE OSBORNE, Cameron's liege and treasurer

DOMINIC CUMMINGS, a wayward campaigning genius

MICHAEL GOVE, Her Majesty's Minister for Justice

BORIS JOHNSON, a law unto himself

NIGEL FARAGE, Leader of the United Kingdom Independence Party

SIR BOB GELDOF, a popular singer now in retirement

DAVID DIMBLEBY, a television broadcaster

SAMANTHA CAMERON, David's wife

JEREMY CORBYN, Leader of Her Majesty's Opposition

SARAH, LADY MACBETH, Michael's wife and newspaper columnist

RACHEL SYLVESTER, a journalist

ANDREA LEADSOM, Minister of State for Energy

THERESA MAY, Her Majesty's Minister for Home Affairs

LIAM FOX, Her Majesty's Minister for International Trade

DAVID DAVIS, Her Majesty's Minister for Leaving the European Union

JEAN-CLAUDE JUNCKER, President of the European Commission

DONALD TUSK, President of the European Council

MICHEL BARNIER, Chief Negotiator for the European Union

FIONA HILL, Theresa May's aide

NICK TIMOTHY, Theresa May's aide

BRENDA, a member of the public

JULIE ETCHINGHAM, a television broadcaster

PHILIP MAY, Theresa May's husband

LORD BUCKETHEAD, a political candidate

PHILIP HAMMOND, the Chancellor of the Exchequer

LEE NELSON, a comedian

JACOB REES-MOGG, Chairman of the European Research Group

SIR GRAHAM BRADY, Chairman of the 1922 Committee

MR SPEAKER, Speaker of the House of Commons

GEOFFREY COX, Conservative politician

DOMINIC RAAB, Her Majesty's Minister for Leaving
the European Union

KENNETH CLARKE, a Conservative politician

SAMMY WILSON, a Democratic Unionist Party politician

MATT HANCOCK, Her Majesty's Minister for Digital and Culture

MARK HARPER, a Conservative politician

JEREMY HUNT, Her Majesty's Minister for Foreign Affairs

SAJID JAVID, Her Majesty's Minister for Home Affairs

ESTHER McVEY, Her Majesty's Minister for Work and Pensions

RORY STEWART, Her Majesty's Minister for International Development

CAMERAMAN, FLUNKEY, AIDES, RETURNING OFFICER,
MILITIA MEN, CROWDS

PROLOGUE

Enter LAURA KUENSSBERG, *BBC Political Editor,*

with a cameraman.

KUENSSBERG   This is our story. All Brexit's a stage,
And all the men and women merely players:
They have their exits and their entrances;
And each one in their time plays crucial parts,
The main roles being seven in number.   5
First, David Cameron, Prime Minister,
Shining of face, imperious manner,
As one for whom rule was seen as birthright.
Eton, and Oxford, and PR (as in
Public Relations, not Proportional   10
Representation), and then a safe seat.
The Cotswolds, no less: Jeremy Clarkson,
And Rebekah Brooks, and that bloke from Blur.
The Chipping Norton set, as they were call'd.
Then Michael Gove, once Cameron's close chum   15
Who set principle in place of friendship
By opposing Dave's own Remain campaign
And in so doing sunder'd their amity.
Perhaps embolden'd by taking down Dave
And with a taste for Old Etonians   20
Mike then set his sights on our third man here.
Boris Johnson. BoJo. Bozza. Boris.

Or Alexander Boris de Pfeffel

To give his full, glorious moniker.

An insatiable, priapic lover,   25

Sighing like furnace, with a woeful ballad

Made to his mistresses' eyebrows (or lower).

Full of strange oaths, hair mess'd like the scarecrow.

Some call him Fool, Jester, national tonic;

Some call him dangerous, unprincipl'd,   30

A man loyal to self and self alone.

Some people call him the space cowboy, yeah

'Cos he speaks with the pompatus of love.

(Prithee excuse me: different song.)

And then comes Farage, Nigel of that ilk,   35

With pint of ale, and cigarette in mouth.

A hearty chap chock-full of bonhomie,

A straight talker, socking it to all those

Dreary PC pinkos with some home truths.

Perhaps a golf club bore with braying laugh   40

And a navy-blue, gold-button'd blazer.

The commodore of the local yacht club

Or fail'd Norfolk DJ Alan Partridge?

'You're racist! Fascist! Dangerous!' cry the

Metropolitan liberal elite.   45

And so he plays his part. Amidst these men

Is the leading lady of our story.

Theresa May. Let me be very clear.

That's what she always says. 'Let me be clear.'

The Maybot, absent human emotion.   50

A weak leader, spineless, inflexible?

(A biological contradiction.)
Or a serious, dutiful woman
Landed with a most impossible task?
A political Sisyphus, pushing 55
Brexit rock up Parliament Hill;
Or Maidenhead's Odysseus, steering her
Course between the Scylla of the EU
And the Charybdis of the ERG.
Across the aisle, Jeremy Corbyn. 60
Darling of the Labour Party grassroots
Loath'd by his parliamentary colleagues.
Magic Grandpa, once student protestor,
Rejecting the Blairite New Labour cult
And taking things back to the olden days 65
When socialism was a viable
Alternative to the capitalists.
An unenthusiastic Remainer
On Brexit itself Jeremy seems torn.
Seeking always to keep his options open 70
And avoid fixing on a position.
And last, JRM of the ERG.
Jacob Rees-Mogg, double-breast'd of suit
Impeccably courteous of manner,
The Honourable Member for the 19th 75
Century, Victorian in attitude,
Sure of the continu'd employment of
'Nanny', loyal family retainer
(As oppos'd to Remainer, God forbid!)
Now charg'd with yet more work as Jacob is 80

Blessèd sixfold with the fruits of his loins
And their extravagant nomenclatures.
Alphege, Wentworth, Somerset, Boniface,
Anselm, Fitzwilliam, Wulfric, Leyson
And Sixtus: all these and more can be found   85
In the register of the Rees-Mogg births.
These are our players: now the events they play.
Long has been the road: longer yet it goes.
We know what has been. What is left to come?
What will be the very last scene of them all,   90
That ends this strange eventful history?
A fine settlement negotiat'd?
A further extension from the EU?
The revoking of Article 50?
Or the crashing out that is a 'no deal'   95
Sans agreement, sans customs union,
Sans single market, sans Irish backstop,
Sans new relationship, sans everything?
Now back to you in the studio, Huw.

[Exit Kuenssberg.

ACT I

SCENE I

Bloomberg Television Headquarters, London. January 2013

Enter DAVID CAMERON, *Prime Minister*
and his liege, GEORGE OSBORNE.

CAMERON　　[*To himself:*] Today I wish to talk about Europe.

OSBORNE　　I really think—

CAMERON　　—Prithee keep thy counsel!
[*Sighs*] You have caus'd me to lose my place. Pray speak.

OSBORNE　　This referendum you are proposing　　　　　5
Is, I fear, not a bad idea.

CAMERON　　Really?

OSBORNE　　It is a terrible idea. The worst.
Of all the bad ideas you've had, and there
Have been some absolute stinkers—　　　　　10

CAMERON　　Such as?

OSBORNE　　That rose garden speech with Nick Clegg, for one.

CAMERON   Fair enough.

OSBORNE   Of all those ideas, this one is
           The worst, and by a considerable   15
           Distance. Worse than all the others combin'd.

CAMERON   Continue.

OSBORNE   Once you start, you lose control.
           Deep runs animosity in the shires
           Toward the whole European project.   20
           These people do not Tweet nor Facebook do
           But their silence is not assent, and nor
           Should we take it as such. A bloody nose
           For Brussels, and for us the government;
           The queue to make that punch is a long one.   25

CAMERON   The fruitcakes, loonies and closet racists?

OSBORNE   The members who desert us for UKIP.
           Call them what you want. They vote agin us.
           They will lap up the honey'd populist
           Words of the nearest pound shop demagogue: 30
           The easy answers to complex questions,
           The cheap cooing of a reckless lover.
           There are those too with genuine concerns:
           Fishermen and farmers both, who buckle
           At the yoke of EU regulation.   35
           Blame the French—

CAMERON   I do. 'Tis good for the soul.

OSBORNE   Aye. There is truth in that, and more beside.
              These are the currents which run beneath us.
              Three problems above all I can foresee.   40

CAMERON   Why speaketh thou like Yoda, with sentence
              Invert'd so the first words are the last?

OSBORNE   The gravity of things to emphasise.
              The first of the problems is as follows.
              In or out? Stay or Leave? All or nothing.   45
              There is no halfway house, no room to move.
              Not further integration on the table
              Nor adopting the single currency.
              'Twere those and we lost, there's still a way back.
              But on membership itself, 'tis all in.   50
              And if all in doth fail, then 'tis all out.
              The second problem I enumerate.
              This will split the Conservative Party
              Clean down the midst, as though a warrior
              Had cleav'd it straight through with a scimitar.   55
              All parties are coalitions, we too.
              Europhobes and Europhiles under one roof.
              The truce is uneasy, but it holds still.
              You call this referendum, and you will
              Cry havoc, and let slip the dogs of war.   60
              Last but not least amongst my vexations
              Are the two Eds.

CAMERON   They are better than one.

OSBORNE   Pray explain.

CAMERON   Two Eds are better than one.   65

OSBORNE   This punning does not become you, my lord.
            Messrs Balls and Miliband are tipping
            Their hats toward the City and business.
            We are the party of business, not they.
            To put this status in clear jeopardy   70
            Would be an act of monstrous foolishness.
            You will let your entire premiership
            Be held hostage to this if you proceed.

CAMERON   The value is in the offer itself.
            We will regain enough members to win,   75
            Or at least to be the largest party.
            Another five years of coalition
            And we can blame the Lib Dems for saying no.
            No referendum as part of joint rule.

OSBORNE   We blame the Lib Dems for everything, no?   80

CAMERON   What else do you think they're there for, my liege?

                    A FLUNKEY *enters.*

FLUNKEY   You're on in ten seconds, Prime Minister.

                                [Exeunt Flunkey and Osborne.

                 CAMERON *goes to a lectern.*

CAMERON   Today I wish to talk about Europe;

                 Its future, and our future, interlinked.

                 'Tis now thirty-eight years since you the public   85

                 Were last ask'd to cast a vote on Europe.

                 It was the Common Market in those days.

                 Now 'tis the European Union.

                 Nine members had the EEC back then;

                 Now there are no fewer than twenty-eight.   90

                 'Tis time to ask the question once again.

                 In the next Conservative government

                 We will give the British people their say.

                 A referendum: simple, binary.

                 To stay in the EU, or to come out.   95

                                [Exit Cameron.

SCENE 2

                 Leave EU Headquarters. Early 2016.

                 Enter KUENSSBERG *with a cameraman.*

KUENSSBERG   The 2015 general election

                 Was too close to call. So said the polls.

They all predicted a hung parliament.

[*Aside:*] Some people would like a hanged parliament.

But the Lib Dems were blam'd for everything   5

Especially raising tuition fees

And their vote went down even quicker than

Cristiano Ronaldo in the box.

Much to everyone's surprise [*Aside:*] probably

his own as well, Cameron won outright.   10

An overall majority of twelve.

He return'd to Number Ten, the die cast.

Now to put the question to the people

And to find once again that the pollsters

Were as useful as a chocolate fireguard.   15

                    [*Exit Kuenssberg.*

                Enter DOMINIC CUMMINGS.

CUMMINGS   Something is rotten in the state of Europe.

Peace be to them, if they in peace permit

Our just and lineal entrance to our own.

No Brussels bureaucrat nor Strasbourg sap

Shall tithe or toll in our dominions;   20

But as we, under Liz, are supreme head,

So, under Liz, that great supremacy

Where we do reign we will alone uphold,

Without th'assistance of a Europe hand.

So tell Juncker, all reverence set apart   25

To him and his usurp'd authority.

O, let us pay the time but needful woe,

Since it hath been beforehand with our griefs.

This England never did, nor never shall,

Lie at the proud foot of a conqueror.   30

And we shall shock them! Nought shall make us rue,

If England to itself do rest but true.

The white cliffs of Dover, that pale-fac'd shore,

Whose foot spurns back the ocean's roaring tides

And coops from other lands her islanders,   35

Even till that England, hedg'd in with the main,

That water-wallèd bulwark, still secure

And confident from foreign purposes.

Remember whom you are to cope withal:

A sort of vagabonds, rascals and runaways,   40

A scum of Belgians and base lackey peasants,

Whom their o'ercloy'd country vomits forth.

Let's whip these stragglers o'er the seas again,

Lash hence these overweening rags of France,

These famish'd beggars, weary of their lives.   45

Fight, gentlemen of England! Fight, bold yeomen!

Draw, archers, draw your arrows to the head!

Advance our standards! Set upon our foes!

Our ancient word of courage, fair Saint George!

O inglorious league of Jean Monnet!   50

Shall we, upon the footing of our land,

Send fair-play orders and make compromise,

Insinuation, parley and base truce

To arms invasive? Not while I have breath.

So, to work. I see people as they are,   55

And not as others might like them to be.

Winning thinking and not wishful thinking.

Immigration, sovereignty and cost;

These three things are what vex people the most.

These are therefore where we must concentrate   60

Our resources, our campaign, our focus.

Close off the borders, make laws in London,

Stop giving so much money to Brussels.

On this tripartite battlefield we stand,

And on this battlefield we shall triumph.   65

Let us give power to the powerless,

Strength unto the weak, returning what they've lost.

Our clarion call, loud and proud and clear.

Take control, take control. Take back control.

[Exit Cummings.

SCENE 3

10 Downing Street.

Enter MICHAEL GOVE *and* DAVID CAMERON.

CAMERON   What vexeth thee, sir?

GOVE   'Tis this Brexit thing.

You and I are friends and allies alike;

Sitting on the front bench of Parliament,

Introducing political reform   5

And having each other round for supper.

My wife is godmother to your daughter.

These bonds, professional and personal,

Are a source of great and real joy to me.

But now my mind is afear'd with disquiet.   10

I am on the horns of a dilemma

For you hoist your flag to the Remain cause

Whereas I believe we should be Leavers.

So now professional and personal

Are in clear opposition within me.   15

My beliefs or my friend? I must choose one

And betray the other: that is the truth.

CAMERON   Thou knowest that if I lose, I resign.

Thou couldst do that to a friend? Seriously?

GOVE   Two years? Hast thou already forgotten?   20

Chief whip, that's what thou made me, with no cause.

The education brief, my most priz'd job,

Full of zeal and fight for radical change.

I lov'd ev'ry minute of my time there.

And you snatch'd it from me as though I were   25

A child caught stealing cake mix from the bowl.

CAMERON   The numbers did not lie. Public sector

Workers disliked both you and your reforms.

I was oblig'd to be a pragmatist

And move you sideways for the greater good.   30

GOVE   'Twas not sideways, though. 'Twas a demotion.

            Gone from Cabinet, and with salary

            Reduc'd by around thirty thousand pounds.

CAMERON   'Tis but a trifle, an amount that small.

GOVE   Thou cannot speak for me on this matter.   35

            I am an adopt'd son, a Scots man;

            A scholarship boy, hidebound by my class.

            No silver spoon, no Old Etonian,

            No Bullingdon tailcoats, no fine champagne.

            We are here together: we are diff'rent.   40

CAMERON   Are we not here still? Number Ten itself

            The seat of power for centuries now.

            We won the election. I was prov'd right.

            Hear me. Thou art Minister for Justice

            And justice thou carry like a great sword.   45

            Thou and I have fought to wrest this party

            From the palsi'd hands of the dinosaurs.

            A new, compassionate Conservatism:

            That is our legacy, if we finish.

            But if I lose, and I go, then all that   50

            Will be lost to the prejudic'd gammons.

GOVE   Gammons? Dost thou speak of the pig's head?

CAMERON   Lies, sir! Lies, lies, lies and damn calumny!

GOVE   Thou hast had no more loyal friend than I.

                I have kept my counsel regarding Europe.   55

                My feelings I have lock'd down in a box,

                But now that box has been thrown wide open.

                Collective responsibility – gone!

                The next box is one in which I must tick

                On the ballot paper, to stay or go.   60

                And beforehand I must declare my side.

                If I come with thou, 'tis most insincere:

                If I go agin thou, 'tis troublesome.

CAMERON   I cannot make this decision for thee.

GOVE   Nor would I ask that of thou, nor anyone.   65

                I have no relish for this choice, nor sauce.

                Thou ask of me what I would not ask back:

                To be a stooge, a butler, a lemming,

                A coward, even, fearful of the hurt.

                This above all – to mine own self be true;   70

                And it must follow, as the night the day,

                Thou canst not then be false to any man.

                                                    [Exeunt.

SCENE 4

An Islington town house.

BORIS JOHNSON *is sitting at a computer. He looks even
more dishevelled than usual.*

JOHNSON   Soon I must nail my colours to the mast.

Not by press conference nor bland statement

But in the *Daily Telegraph* broadsheet,

Which pays me handsomely for a column

Every Monday morning, start of the week.   5

Quarter of a million pounds per year?

You might think that. To quote Francis Urquhart,

I couldn't possibly comment. (Perhaps

more *ego potissimum commendet*;

Nothing says 'Bozza' like a Latin bomb.)   10

But which way shall I turn? Which path the best

For my country, my party and myself?

[*Aside:*] Not necessarily in that order.

The colour of mine self doth come and go

Between my purpose and my conscience,   15

Like heralds 'twixt two dreadful battles set.

My passion is so ripe it needs must break.

As a young lad I wish'd to be 'World King',

A yearning which still burns strong in my breast.

I have hid that lamp beneath my bushel;   20

But now the spotlight is upon us all.

Choose wisely, and the ball may yet come free

From the back of the scrum for me to score.

Be injudicious, and mark yet more time.

To leave or not to leave, that is the question: 25

Whether 'tis nobler in the mind to suffer

The slings and arrows of outrag'd Remainers,

Or to take arms against a sea of Leavers,

And by opposing end them? To leave, to stay,

No more; and by leaving to say we end   30
The EU, and the thousand petty rules
That we adhere to, – 'tis a consummation
Devoutly to be wish'd. To stay, to leave;
To stay, perchance to leave: ay, there's the rub;
For in that move to leave what dreams may come,   35
When we have shuffl'd off this Brussels yoke,
Must give us pause: there's the respect
That makes calamity of membership;
For who would bear the Brussels whips and scorns,
The bureaucrat's wrong, the mandarin's contumely,   40
The pangs of lost control, the law's delay,
The insolence of office, and the spurns
That patient merit of the unworthy takes,
When he himself might his quietus make
With a bare bodkin? who would these fardels bear,   45
To grunt and sweat under a weary life,
But that the dread of something after Leave –
The undiscover'd country, from whose bourn
No traveller returns – puzzles the will,
And makes us rather bear those ills we have   50
Than fly to others that we know naught of?
Thus conscience does make cowards of us all;
And thus the native hue of resolution
Is sickli'd o'er with the pale cast of thought;
And enterprises of great pith and moment,   55
With this regard, their currents turn awry,
And lose the name of action.

He rises and begins to pace the room.

Ach! 'Tis so hard.
Let me enumerate, for and against,
And find a way through this confus'd thicket.   60
First, to Leave. What is the EU if not
An anti-democratic behemoth?
Invisible government, by stealth
Making our laws, our decisions, our lives.
Never elect'd, nay accountable.   65
Building a kennel round this fine bulldog,
At first muzzling him, then neutering him.
We must kick down this kennel while we can,
Or else we will soon find it too secure
Fixing us like flies in amber [*Aside*]: not Rudd.   70
This ever-closer union scares me;
This lust for regulation is obscene.
As Mayor of Londinium, I was forc'd
To watch helplessly as cyclists perish'd;
Unseen by pantechnicons while they turn'd.   75
Blind spots on trucks. An easy, quick thing to fix.
Nay, said Brussels. The lorries fully conform
To our regulations, and can't be chang'd.
Nothing could I nor the government do.
A great city, a great country, stripp'd of   80
Plenipotentiary authority.
We cannot stop this machine from inside;
We can merely jam a temporary
And occasional spoke in the ratchet.

PM Dave went to renegotiate   85

With Brussels, Berlin, Juncker and Merkel.

To probe the swollen belly of the beast

And return with British sovereignty,

Like Hercules bringing Eurydice

Back from the underworld to great Blighty.   90

Powers repatriat'd one by one –

Fisheries, farming, the social chapter –

Political hostages returning home.

Ring the church bells! Build bonfires on beacons!

Fly the union flag from ev'ry steeple!   95

Let peasants drink themselves insensible

On non-EU-approv'd moonshine scrumpy!

Let bards compose songs to the many glories

Of David Cameron, British hero!

Alack, 'twas not to be. Concessions? Minor.   100

All sound and fury, signifying nothing.

For EU law is an incoming tide.

It flows into estuaries, up rivers.

Supreme, irreversible, unheld back,

And flooding out national discretion.   105

We are passengers lock'd in a taxi;

Satnav wonky, driver no speak English,

Taking us to the wrong destination.

Their ideal is one which we do not share:

A union, *e pluribus unum*.   110

We should be 'of' Europe but not 'in' it.

Interest'd, even associat'd,

But still neither compris'd, nor compromis'd,

Nor infantilis'd by Nanny Brussels.

Quarter of the earth was once our empire.   115

A great country we were, and still we are.

In how many fields do we lead Europe?

Financial services, the media,

Universities, biosciences,

The arts and tech and manufacturing.   120

Legion are our exports, above all this;

British parliament'ry democracy,

Our electing lawmakers to power

And removing them through ballot-box same.

A pause.

Now, to Remain. What is leaving, if not   125

a bit cranky, and sepia-tint'd;

a little cravat-wearing pass-the-port?

A harking back to a most golden age

Which maybe never even existed?

What will be the economic fallout?   130

The pound in freefall, the markets crashing?

What of the Union if England says Leave,

But bonny Scotland chooses Remain?

There's too much at stake. There's too much unknown.

Shut your eyes. Hold your breath. Think of Britain.   135

Think of the EU. Think of the future.

Think of your children and grandchildren

Living and working all over Europe;

selling things, making friends, finding partners.

This great European project is flaw'd.   140

But it is also all we have, for now.

Both pro-Europe and pro-rest of the world;

That should be our policy, as with cake,

Both pro-having it and pro-eating it.

He weighs up the arguments and comes to a sudden decision.

I cannot do this. I cannot traduce   145

This royal throne of kings, this sceptr'd isle,

This earth of majesty, this seat of Mars,

This other Eden, demi-paradise;

This fortress built by Nature for herself,

Against infection and the hand of war,   150

This happy breed of men, this little world,

This precious stone set in the silver sea,

Which serves it in the office of a wall,

Or as a moat defensive to a house,

Against the envy of less happier lands;   155

This bless'd plot, this earth, this realm, this England,

This nurse, this teeming womb of royal kings,

Fear'd by their breed, and famous by their birth.

To the people I trust sovereignty

For they alone are truly sovereign.   160

And in this matter they will get it right.

My mind is made, my die is cast. I have

Come off the fence with deafening éclat.

He goes to the window and looks out.

I am for Boris, first, middle, and last;

Me, myself and I, as De La Soul sang.   165

But of course one cannot say so out loud.

I declare myself for great principle.

I am for Leave, and leave this house I must.

There are hundreds waiting for me below

'Tis truly an imperial goatfuck.   170

                                              [*Exit.*

SCENE 5

Enter KUENSSBERG *with a cameraman.*

KUENSSBERG   Two households, both alike in dignity,

In fair Britannia, where we lay our scene,

From ancient grudge break to new mutiny,

Where civil blood makes civil hands unclean.

From forth the staunch camps of these two foes,   5

Come anger, vitriol and gross discord.

All the unsettl'd humours of the land –

Rash, inconsiderate, fiery voluntaries,

With twist'd faces and fierce dragons' spleens.

And as I travell'd hither through the land,   10

I found the people strangely fantasi'd,

Possess'd with rumours, full of idle dreams,

Not knowing what they fear, but full of fear.

Project Fear, so said the many Leavers,

Brushing off dark catastrophic warnings   15

Of an economic Armageddon.

Stronger, Safer, Better Off, said Remain:

Now is not the time to leap in the dark.

Heed ye not the empty Leave promises;

They bring smooth comforts false, worse than true

    wrongs.   20

O world, thy slippery turns! Friends now fast sworn,

Whose double bosoms seem to wear one heart,

Whose hours, whose bed, whose meal and exercise

Are still together, who twin, as 't were, in love

Unseparable, shall within this hour,   25

On a dissension of a doit, break out

To bitterest enmity: so, fellest foes,

Whose passions and whose plots have broke their sleep

To take the one the other, by some chance,

Some trick not worth an egg, shall grow dear friends 30

And in doing interjoin their issues.

This is the two hours' traffic of our stage.

The which if you with patient ears attend,

What here shall miss, our toil shall strive to mend.

But, soft! what light through yonder window breaks? 35

It is the east, and Obama is the sun!

He cometh with slow diction, grave warning:

'You think you can just cut trade deals with us?

Perhaps you may heed the President here,

Who will tell thee of our clear intentions.   40

A trade agreement between thee and we?

Just the two of us, as Bill Withers sang?

Maybe, but not for the longest of times.

Our focus is on the vast EU bloc;

More than half a billion people there.   45

This is our priority and effort;

You guys will be in the back of the queue.'

Project Fear, cri'd Leave again. Project Fear!

This man hates Britain. The bust of Churchill

Which had long adorn'd the Oval Office,   50

He did remove. Part Kenyan, they muttered;

A hater of the British Empire and

Churchill's most vehement defence thereof.

How dare he come and deign to lecture us?

Away, Barack! Avast with you and   55

Your condescension, your patronising.

From Gove, the quote of the entire campaign:

'The people have had enough of experts;

I'm afear'd it is time to say: "You're fir'd!"'

The Leavers, undaunt'd, kept on going;   60

Their message proclaim'd over and over.

Immigration. Sovereignty. Turkey.

The establishment ramparts they assail'd.

'Three hundred and fifty million pounds.'

A figure, on a bus. 'How much we give   65

To the EU every single week.'

'Foul!' cri'd Remainers. 'That's the gross figure.

You must include rebates and investment.'

'Three hundred and fifty million pounds.

Let's give it to the NHS instead.' 70

Breaking Point, said a poster of migrants.

'Foul!' cri'd Remainers again and again.

We can all get along. Publish we this peace

To all our people. Set we forward: let

An EU and a British ensign wave 75

Friendly together: so through these towns march:

And in the temple of great superstate

Our peace we'll ratify; seal it with feasts.

Set on there! Never was a war did cease,

Ere bloody hands were wash'd, with such a peace. 80

[Exit Kuenssberg.

SCENE 6

The River Thames. A flotilla of fishing boats
with pro-Brexit banners approaches.

Enter NIGEL FARAGE, *resplendent in naval blazer.*

FARAGE   I am a fisherman. Get a small boat,

Sod off into the Channel, land some bass.

Peace and quiet: no calls, no interruption.

But new EU rules prevent even this.

For me, 'tis sport. For thousands, 'tis their life. 5

An island nation we are, with waters;

Without control of such, we are nothing.

A pleasure cruiser passes Farage's.

Enter SIR BOB GELDOF *and* AIDE.

GELDOF   Fuck the address. Give them the phone number.

Give us your fucking money.

AIDE   Sire, we are   10

No longer at Live Aid. This is Brexit.

GELDOF   Gadzooks! Pass me the loudhailer, kind sir.

GELDOF *raises the loudhailer.*

[*To Farage:*] Farage! You are no fisherman's friend!

When you were appoint'd to a priz'd seat

On the European Parliament   15

Fisheries Committee, your attendance –

Perhaps you could tell us what it was like?

Answer comes there none. Let me jog your mind.

Forty-three meetings you could have gone to.

You turn'd up to just one. Did you lose your way?   20

You are a fraud. Go back down the river;

You are up one sans canoe and sans paddle.

The two armadas exchange hose fire before a police launch interposes
itself between them. Geldof and his supporters turn the music up
and begin flicking V-signs at Farage's protesters.

FARAGE   Disgusting! Absolutely disgusting!

                [Aside, to an aide:] This will play so well in the press.

                    Trust me.

                We protest against the establishment;   25

                The establishment protests against us.

                                                        [Exeunt.

SCENE 7

10 Downing Street.

Enter CAMERON *and his team. They are watching the results on TV.*

There's footage of FARAGE *appearing at a Leave party interspersed with*
        DAVID DIMBLEBY *announcing the results of the Referendum.*

FARAGE   *[Within:]* Win or lose this battle, we have done it.

                We will win this war, get this country back;

                And we will get our independence back,

                Our borders as well. This is a great day.

            CAMERON's *face is unreadable as the results come in.*

DIMBLEBY   *[Within:]* To Sunderland now, a bellwether result;   5

                A sixty-forty Leave victory is due.

                More than that, and Remain are in trouble.

                Now live to the Returning Officer…

RETURNING [*Within:*] All the votes cast in favour of Remain:
OFFICER
     Fifty-one thousand, nine hundred thirty.   10

     All votes cast for Leave: eighty-two thousand…

     An eruption of noise on the TV.

DIMBLEBY [*Within:*] That makes sixty-one per cent for the Leavers;
     More than was forecast. A nationwide shift
     Would see Leave carry the Referendum.

     CAMERON *rubs his face with his hands.*

FARAGE [*Within:*] Dare to dream that the dawn is breaking on 15
     An independent United Kingdom.
     This will be a vict'ry for real people,
     Ordinary people, decent people,
     Without a single bullet being fir'd.

DIMBLEBY [*Within:*] It is six am. Vote Leave have secur'd 20
     More than half the votes cast, and have triumph'd.
     The most extraordinary of moments.
     [Exeunt Farage, Dimbleby and Returning Officer.

     CAMERON *winces. Enter* OSBORNE.

CAMERON What say you, my liege? How call you this night?

OSBORNE Well, you're fuck'd, I'm fuck'd and the country's fuck'd.

CAMERON   Aye, I fear that's about the size of it.   25

[Exeunt.

ACT II

SCENE 1

An empty lectern stands outside 10 Downing Street.

Enter CAMERON with his wife Samantha. He walks to the lectern.

CAMERON   The British people have vot'd to leave.
                An instruction that must be deliver'd;
                Their will must be completely respect'd.
                I fought directly and passionately
                For what I think and feel – head, heart and soul.   5
                But now we all must take a diff'rent path.
                I will do my best to steady the ship
                Of state over the coming weeks and months.
                But it would not be right for me to try
                To be the captain in the longer term.   10
                Someone else must be the one chosen to
                Steer Britain to its next destination.

His voice begins to crack with emotion.

                I love this country. To have serv'd it has
                Been an honour truly beyond compare.
                Even more so than being made house captain   15
                At Eton. Some of you know I went there.
                More so, still, than being elect'd to
                The posh boys' Bullingdon Club at Oxford;

Where we wore tailcoats, and got very drunk,
And smash'd up restaurants, and abused people.   20
No damage that money could not put right.
'Buller! Buller! Buller!' That, our war cry;
Me, and Osborne, and of course Boris too.
And now we are in charge of the country.
What else did you expect, bar destruction?   25

He recovers his poise.

I will do all I can to help Britain,
To see it thriving, vibrant, great again;
But in the meantime I intend to spend
More time with my many directorships,
And chillaxing in a fine shepherd's hut,   30
Writing my memoirs, playing Fruit Ninja.
A game of tennis, a spot of pub lunch.
In years to come Mr Danny Dyer,
Who stars in the popular *EastEnders*,
Will proclaim that I have my 'trotters up'.   35
'Twat!' he will say, on morning TV. 'Twat!'
The clip will go viral; hate me you will.
He will capture the mood of a nation.
The heir to Blair, I did once call myself.
Blair did good things, but Iraq's what will be   40
Writ on his tombstone, eternal legacy.
Good things did I too, and like him condemn'd;
The man who call'd the vote, gambl'd and lost.
But I leave you with one firm prediction.

Whoever takes my place, within six months,   45
You will hark back to my premiership
As a golden age of style, competence,
Leadership and responsibility.
Whosoever follows will make me look
Like Churchill, William the Conqueror,   50
Boadicea and Hugh Grant in that film –
You know, Christmas, love, soppy – Combin'd.
Right, that's your lot. I will take no questions.
The Jeremy Kyle Show's starting in five
And after that, *Homes Under the Hammer*.   55

[Exeunt.

SCENE 2

The Labour Party headquarters.

Enter KUENSSBERG *with a cameraman.*

KUENSSBERG   'Twas not just the Conservative Party
Seeking a change at the top. Labour, too.
Invisible, lacklustre, tepid, wan;
All these, and more, were said about the role
Of Jeremy Corbyn in the campaign.   5
A Remainer, he had proclaim'd himself;
A submarine of that ilk, truth be told,
Barely surfacing to support the cause.
His shadow cabinet were none too pleas'd.

Heidi Alexander (health) resign'd first   10
At breakfast time, Corbyn's soya latte
And organic cornflakes barely consum'd.
Gloria De Piero (young people)
Came next, at the hour of elevenses;
Just past midday, Ian Murray (Scotland);   15
Lilian Greenwood (transport) at lunchtime;
Then Kerry McCarthy (environment),
And quick, Seema Malhotra (Treasury);
Teatime: Lucy Powell (education).
Now to Vernon Coaker (Northern Ireland),   20
Past seven: Charlie Falconer (Justice)
Then came Karl Turner (Attorney Gen'ral).
Finally, Chris Bryant (Commons leader),
Saying 'If you refuse to step aside
I fear you will go down in history as   25
the man who did break the Labour Party.'
Eleven folk gone in thirteen hours.
Now back to you in the studio, Huw.

[Exit Kuenssberg.

Enter CORBYN, *an ageing figure not dissimilar to Lear, with his* AIDE.

AIDE   Sire, we have news of more resignations.

CORBYN   How many?   30

AIDE   Sixty-five. Your front-bench posts
        Cannot all be fill'd. We need more members.

One hundred and seventy-two members
Have express'd their no confidence in thee.
Just forty members stand loyal with thee.   35

CORBYN   The party faithful are with me, pray tell?

AIDE   Indeed they are, sire. Only they can shun you.
             You will win a leadership election.
             Momentum, and the grassroots, are for you.
             The parliament'ry members are at sea.   40
             Candidate have they none, nor programme too.

CORBYN   I thank Ed Miliband. He chang'd the rules
             Allowing new members to cast a vote.
             We are a socialist haven once more
             As Labour should always be.   45

AIDE   The clue's in
             The name. Labour. Newly without the 'New'.

CORBYN   Aye, 'tis so. Then send a communiqué.
             Tell them that Jeremy Corbyn is the
             Democratic'lly elected leader   50
             Of the Labour Party, and that is how
             He will remain.

AIDE   'Tis the first for some time.

CORBYN   Prithee, explain.

AIDE	That you speak loud 'Remain'.
CORBYN	Aide, dost thou wish to become an ex-aide?
AIDE	Nay, sire.
CORBYN	Then I prithee, keep thy counsel.
AIDE	Aye, sire.
CORBYN	Tell them I am going nowhere.
	Apart, perchance, to see my allotment.
	And to the Socialist Workers' meeting
	On the Seven Sisters Road at seven.
AIDE	Try saying that when you've had a few meads.
CORBYN	I abjure alcohol, as well you know.
AIDE	I fear we will all need more alcohol,
	Not less, ere this whole Brexit is finish'd.

55

60

65

[Exeunt.

SCENE 3

The Hurlingham Club. A party full of revelry.

Enter JOHNSON *and* GOVE. *They talk in a corner.*

GOVE   We submit your credentials tomorrow;

             For leader, for Prime Minister, for all.

             All candidates must declare themselves then.

             Only two titans are there running, in truth;

             Thou, and Theresa of the Home Office.   5

             The others are makeweights and also-rans.

             But Mrs Leadsom, Andrea by name,

             She doth concern me.

JOHNSON   Relax, my old fruit!

             Leave Leadsom to old Bozza. No, you hound!   10

             Not in that way, though my reputation

             Doth, I confess, precede me in such things.

             I have ensur'd that she will cause no harm.

GOVE   How, sir?

JOHNSON   By promising a top-three role.   15

GOVE   Hast thou forgotten the same promise made

             To me, as the price of my true support?

JOHNSON   To the contrary, good squire. Three there are.

             Deputy prime minister, chancellor,

             And the chief Brexit negotiator.   20

             You shall have one, and Leadsom another.

GOVE   Perchance to join the first and third of those?

JOHNSON   A topic for discussion, certainly.

GOVE   With me onside, the *Daily Mail* follows.

The editor is sceptical of you;   25

But my wife writes for them, and he trusts her.

Daily Mail: the voice of Middle England.

JOHNSON   *Angliam mediam vocem*, rather.

GOVE   Middle England does not much Latin do.

You have become *un vrai homme sérieux*   30

As they say across La Manche in Paris.

Your role in the Leave campaign was crucial

In helping us triumph against the odds.

Many qualities have I, but not this:

Your charisma, your charm, your bonhomie.   35

Thou makes folk laugh, sunny smiles in winter.

'Tis a rare, precious gift which we must use.

Were this now association football,

I would be the strong midfield playmaker;

Organis'd, industrious, well-plac'd   40

At all times to advance our noble cause

While thwarting all enemy skirmishes.

Thou would be Cristiano Ronaldo;

Flash, fleet of foot, hairstyle magnificent,

Scoring wonder goals, the crowd's applause thine.   45

Complement'ry roles for well-match'd talents.

Prithee, tell: hast thou made thy promise firm?

JOHNSON   To Leadsom?

GOVE   Aye, to her.

JOHNSON   I did pledge this.   50
            That I would a confirming letter send
            To her in private; and, more, in public
            Hasten myself to the Twitter network,
            And Tweet the pact we have agreed, the two,
            By way of clear record for all to see.   55

GOVE   You have done these things already?

JOHNSON   No, sir.
            I will do them by eight o'clock.

GOVE   Why then?

JOHNSON   That is the deadline she and I agreed.   60

            GOVE *looks at his watch. His face is horror-struck.*

GOVE   'Tis ten past the hour of eight already.

JOHNSON   This cannot be so!

GOVE   This is extremely so!
            She will think you have truly betray'd her.

JOHNSON   She knows I am not the betraying kind.   65

GOVE   Leadsom will run now, I feel sure of it.
           She will regard the deal you made as void;
           And that thou hast, in parlance, stitched her up.
           She will call thou 'Singer, sewing machine.'
           She will run, and she will gain much support.   70
           The grassroots love you, the parliament'ry
           Members very substantially less so.
           'Tis the latter who vote in the last two.
           Leadsom will queer the pitch, and no mistake.

JOHNSON   My confidence remains undimm'd by this.   75

GOVE   Your confidence may be misplac'd in this.
           Let me leave, to consider our next move.
           I bid thee au revoir.

JOHNSON   Not adieu, I hope.

                                        [Exit Gove.

           Let me have men about me that are fat;   80
           Sleek-headed men, and such as sleep o'nights.
           Yond Govester has a lean and hungry look;
           He thinks too much: such men are dangerous.
           Fuck, fuck, fuck. What do we do? Fuck, fuck, fuck.
           Pish! 'Tis I who think too much. 'Twill be fine.   85

                                        [Exit Johnson.

SCENE 4

Gove's town house, North Kensington.

Enter GOVE *with his wife* SARAH, LADY MACBETH
of the Daily Mail.

GOVE He is a man always disappointing;
Not today, perchance, not even tomorrow,
But sooner or later he lets you down.
Incompetent, a shambles, forgetful;
I cannot work with a man much like that.   5
Dave and George, whate'er their faults, were as one;
They fought, yes, but always made their own peace,
And in private first. A unified front
To the world, at all times, in all places.
Could I be as such with Boris? Absurd!   10
'I think this man is ready to lead us.'
My words, tomorrow, ere I withdraw them.
Say them, and be held to them forever.
Coronations are for monarchs alone.
Those who knew Gordon Brown was not the man,   15
Held their peace, and find it held agin them.
To the truth I must for myself be true.

SARAH You can support him no longer, that's clear.

GOVE Aye, 'tis clear. But then whom?

SARAH There is but one.   20

GOVE Theresa?

SARAH Nay, thrice nay. Nor Leadsom.

GOVE Stephen Crabb? With his way-too-tidy beard?

SARAH Nay, for sure. Nor Liam Fox, Doctor Fox.

GOVE He is at least a real doctor, unlike 25
    The Capital Radio disc jockey
    Of similar moniker, 'Doctor Fox'.

SARAH Aye, and that Dr Fox would make more sense
    As leader than the one still in the race.

GOVE But if not Leadsom, nor Boris, nor May, 30
    Nor Crabb nor Fox – then who?

SARAH The mirror shows.

GOVE Me?

SARAH Of course! Who else? To Downing Street!

GOVE 'Tis impossible. A plaisanterie. 35
    Oft have I been asked, oft have I said nay.

SARAH   'Tis the best – nay, the only – solution.

                 Thou hast the experience, the intellect.

                 Thou art filled with substance and gravity.

                 Thou art a reformer, a zealot e'en.   40

                 Thou hast done the Referendum campaign;

                 Long hours, and pressure, and much vitriol,

                 And thou hast been bloodi'd but still unbow'd.

                 The prize is there, thine to take if thou will.

                 A chalice, glittering with sheer promise.   45

GOVE   Chalices can also be most poison'd.

SARAH   Aye, but the poison can also be drawn out.

                 Thou went agin Dave, and thou wast prov'd right.

                 Roll the die once more. Follow thine instincts.

                 Thou must look like the innocent flower,   50

                 But thou must be the serpent beneath it.

GOVE   All causes shall give way: I am now in blood

                 Stepp'd in so far that, should I wade no more,

                 Returning were as tedious as go o'er.

SARAH   Aye, 'tis that spirit! Thou must have no spur   55

                 To prick the sides of thy intent, but only

                 Vaulting ambition, which o'erleaps itself

                 And falls on the other.

GOVE   'Tis not so easy.

                 O, full of scorpions is now my mind.   60

Confusion now hath made his masterpiece.

False face must hide what the false heart doth know.

SARAH   One may smile, and smile, and be a villain;

To the world, that is, but true to thyself.

GOVE   When sorrows come, they come not single spies   65

But in battalions. Stars, hide your fires!

Let not light see my black and deep desires.

SARAH   Make it quick, with no warning nor waver.

GOVE   Is this a dagger which I see before me,

The handle toward my hand? Come, let me clutch thee;   70

I have thee not, and yet I see thee still.

Art thou not, fatal vision, sensible

To feeling as to sight? Or art thou but

A dagger of the mind, a false creation,

Proceeding from the heat-oppress'd brain?   75

I see thee yet, in form as palpable

As this which now I draw.

SARAH   'Tis good. 'Tis right.

[Exeunt.

SCENE 5

Enter BORIS JOHNSON *in the back of a car.*

His mobile rings.

JOHNSON   Govester! Today's the day we make our pitch.

GOVE   [*Within:*] Good sir, I must tell you this. I'm running.

JOHNSON   Splendid! I too am partial to a jog;
               A few miles through the park with heart rate up,
               And lactic burning the legs till they hurt.   5
               Clears the mind, I always find.

GOVE   [*Within:*] Nay, I mean—

JOHNSON   That endorphin high, it can't be beaten.
               'Cept perhaps by illegal narcotics,
               Which you and I would never take, of course;   10
               Or perchance as well by country matters.

GOVE   [*Within:*] I'm running for leader.

JOHNSON   Thou art running my campaign for leader.

GOVE   [*Within:*] I was running your campaign for leader.
               Now I am running for leader myself.   15

               JOHNSON *is silent for a while.*

JOHNSON   Theresa May will be Prime Minister.

GOVE   [*Within:*] That outcome is not within mine purview.

JOHNSON   Why, Govester? Why hast thou abandon'd me?

GOVE   [*Within:*] For the same reasons Leadsom is running.

              I wanted to believe in thee, Boris.   20

              But thou hast let me down more often than

              A flat tyre on an old velocipede.

              Look behind: you might see more detraction

              At your heels than fortunes are before you.

JOHNSON   Thine forward voice is to speak well of me;   25

              Thine backward voice is to utter foul speeches.

GOVE   [*Within:*] I wish thee best of British in thy run.

              JOHNSON *hangs up. He stares into space.*

JOHNSON   As Caesar loved me, I weep for him;

              As he was fortunate, I rejoice at it;

              As he was valiant, I honour him;   30

              But as he was ambitious, I slew him.

              There are tears for his love, joy for his fortune,

              Honour for his valour, and death for his ambition.

              Suddenly angry, he grabs his mobile and dials.

GOVE   [*Within:*] Leave a message after the tone(y Blair).

JOHNSON   [*Shouting*] You starv'ling, you eel-skin, you dried
            neat's-tongue   35
        You bull's-pizzle, you stock-fish! O for breath
        To utter what is like thee! You tailor's-yard,
        You sheath, you bow-case, you vile standing tuck!
        You poor, base, rascally, cheating lack-linen mate!
        Scullion! Rampallian! Fustilarian!   40
        Thou art a boil, a plague sore, an emboss'd
        Carbuncle in my steep corrupt'd blood.
        Thou trunk of humours, hutch of beastliness,
        Swollen parcel of dropsies, bombard of sack,
        Stuffed cloak-bag of guts, roasted Manningtree ox   45
        Thou reverend vice, grey iniquity!
        Thou elvish-mark'd, abortive, rooting hog!
        Thou art a very notable coward,
        An infinite and endless liar, an
        Hourly promise breaker, the owner of   50
        No one good quality. Foul-spoken coward,
        That thund'rest with thy tongue, and with thy
        Weapon nothing dares perform. Thou art a
        Base, proud, shallow, beggarly, three-suited,
        Hundred-pound, filthy worsted-stocking knave;   55
        A lily-liver'd, action-taking, whoreson,
        Glass-gazing, superserviceable, finical rogue;
        One-trunk-inheriting slave; one that wouldst
        Be a bawd in way of good service, and
        Art nothing but the composition of   60
        A knave, beggar, coward, pandar, and the
        Son and heir of a mongrel bitch. I am sick

When I do look on thee. Away! Thou rag,

Thou quantity, thou remnant. There's small choice

In rotten apples. Go, you mouldy rogue!   65

Go, prick thy face, and over-red thy fear.

The rankest compound of villainous smell

That ever offend'd both mine nostrils.

Thy tongue outvenoms all the worms of Nile.

Would thou wert clean enough to spit upon.   70

I desire we may be better strangers.

You are as candle, the better burnt out.

Heaven truly knows that thou art false as hell,

Thou subtle, perjur'd, false, disloyal man!

Dissembling harlot, thou art false in all;   75

No more faith in thee than in a stew'd prune.

The tartness of thy face could sour ripe grapes.

There is a long beep.

ELECTRONIC   [*Within:*] The voicemail memory is full. Goodbye.
VOICE

The car has arrived at its destination. JOHNSON *gets
out and enters a room, where supporters rise and cheer.
He goes to a lectern and waits for them to quieten.*

JOHNSON   To stand tall in the world. To keep us great.

That is the agenda for whoever   80

Has the single honour of leading us.

He slaps his hand twice on the lectern for emphasis, looks down
and then slowly raises his head, jutting out his jaw in his
best Churchill impression.

But I must tell you, my friends, that person
cannot be me.

The room erupts in pandemonium.

[*Exit Johnson.*

Enter CAMERON.

CAMERON   Should have stuck with me, mate.

[*Exeunt.*

SCENE 6

Enter KUENSSBERG *with a cameraman.*

KUENSSBERG   Then were five: Crabb, Fox, Gove, Leadsom and May.
               Crabb and Fox went early, without troubling
               The scorers too much. So to the third round.
               Gove, treachery unforgiven by most;
               A sparse forty-six. Eighty-four for Leadsom;   5
               And for May, one hundred and ninety-nine.
               'Oh dear,' said she on learning this. 'One short.'
               Never satisfi'd, and not bad at maths.
               So now to the grassroots: May versus Leadsom.

Ken Clarke, microphone still on, opining: 10
'Theresa's a bloody difficult woman.'
Maggie's spirit, now reincarnat'd.
For Andrea Leadsom, the news of her
CV: economical with the truth.
Investment fund managing director,   15
She had claim'd. Not so. The truth was more this:
Investment fund marketing director.
Controll'd City funds worth billions? Nay.
Never manag'd funds, nor clients advis'd.
Sarah Palin? Perchance Walter Mitty?   20
High claims now seem flaky, untrustworthy.
But for Leadsom the worst was yet to come.
Now back to you in the studio, Huw.

                                   [*Exit Kuenssberg.*

Enter LEADSOM. *She is being interviewed by*
     RACHEL SYLVESTER *of* The Times.

SYLVESTER   Theresa May hath spoken movingly
              Of the fact that children were not to be.   25
              For her, and for her husband Philip,
              'Twas a source of great, profound sadness.
              But she accepts the hand life has dealt her.
              Thou hast spoken of thy large family,
              And life as both mother and grandmother.   30
              How doth family make thy politics?

LEADSOM   Of over-close acquaintance we are not,

Theresa and I. Sadness must be hers.

But motherhood brings a very real stake

In the future of this sceptr'd isle.   35

She hath nieces, nephews, lots of people:

I have children who too will have children,

And will be a part of what happens next.

[Exeunt.

The next day.

Enter LEADSOM *holding a copy of* The Times.

LEADSOM   'Being a mother gives me edge on May.'

I stand appall'd! I said no such thing at all.   40

Disgusting, despicable, so hateful;

Journalism not so much from the gutter

As from the sewer which runs beneath it.

I demand this of thee: provide the transcript.

The transcript appears.

SYLVESTER   [*Within:*] All the things I said that you said, you said. 45

Thou Tweet thine outrage at my truth-telling;

Others Tweet theirs at thy graceless remarks.

'Vile,' says Alan Duncan (not from *Macbeth*).

'Not PM material,' says Anna Soubry.

'Do us all a favour and step aside.'   50

LEADSOM   Nine weeks' contest? Most undesirable!

We need a new Prime Minister, and now.

I stand aside for Theresa, unmatch'd.

[Exeunt.

SCENE 7

Outside 10 Downing Street.

The removal men are packing up the CAMERONS' *stuff.*

Enter CAMERON.

CAMERON   'Tis my last day in office. My business:

Meetings with ministerial colleagues

In the morning. At midday, PMQs,

Where I shall remind Jeremy Corbyn

That both our houses do leadership choose.   5

We've had resignation, nomination,

competition and coronation. And they?

Haven't even decid'd the rules yet!

When it comes to women prime ministers,

I'm very pleas'd to be able to say: 10

'Pretty soon, it's going to be two–nil.'

He is naught if not resilient, though;

Like the Black Knight of Monty Python, aye.

Kick'd and batter'd: ''tis only a flesh wound!'

Then, an audience with the Queen apart,   15

My afternoon diary is rather clear.

'Tis done. I will miss the roar of the crowd,

Will miss the barbs from the Opposition,

But I will be willing all of you on.

Naught is impossible given the will.   20

As ere I said, I was the future once.

He walks back through the famous black door, humming a tune, and is gone.

[Exit Cameron.

Enter THERESA MAY.

MAY   A daughter of the manse am I, for life.

The Young Conservatives I eschewed

To attend a vicars and tarts party.

You may know me by the things I am not.   25

I am not a showy politician;

I don't tour television studios;

I don't gossip about people at lunch;

I don't go drinking in Parliament's bars;

I don't often wear my heart on my sleeve;   30

I don't do deals. I am professional;

I just get on with the job before me.

No more chumocracy or Notting Hill,

Old Etonian sofa government.

To you, the nation, I pledge this today.   35

Brexit means Brexit. To put it diff'rently,

Brexit means Brexit. Backwards, upside down,

Or in the mirror, Brexit means Brexit.

And we will succeed on behalf of all.

We Conservatives and Unionists –   40
That is the full title of my party –
Value and believe in the union.
England, Scotland, Wales and Northern Ireland;
Precious bonds between nations and peoples;
Every citizen, whoever you are,   45
Wherever you live, whatever you do.
I wish to fight the burning injustices.
If you're poor, you will die nine years early.
If you're black, you will likely be treat'd
Harshly when facing criminal justice.   50
If you're white, and working class, and a boy,
University may not be for you.
If you're at a state school, the top professions
Will more oft be fill'd by private schools.
If you're a woman, you earn less than men.   55
If you suffer from mental health problems,
There's not enough help to hand, and 'tis wrong.
If you're young, you may never own a home.
You have a job, but no security.
You have a house, but can't pay the mortgage.   60
You can just about manage, but no more.
To fight these, to reduce iniquity,
And make a country fit for ev'ryone;
'Tis my goal, and I shan't rest ere 'tis done.
Let us rise to the challenge before us.   65
Let's leave the European Union,
Forge a new role ourselves in the world;
Bold, new, positive. A better Britain.

MAY *goes inside the building, where* GOVE, JOHNSON,
OSBORNE, FOX *and* DAVID DAVIS *are waiting.*

MAY   Fie, let us haste to get this over with.

                This night of the long stiletto knives   70

                As though pluck'd from my kitten leopard heels.

                To you first, Iago Gove – Iagove.

GOVE   A most excellent pun, Prime Minister.

MAY   Flattery, like treachery, thrills me not.

                I quote to you the words of the O'Jays.   75

                'They want to take your place, the backstabbers.'

                Sing with me!

                They all break into song, briefly.

                Enough! No Gareth Malone

                Am I; but thou art now Michael Alone.

GOVE   Another fine pun, Prime Minister.   80

MAY   Perchance I have been a smidgeon unfair.

GOVE   Prime Minister?

MAY   No backstabber, thou.

                Thou didst with force stab Boris in the front,

                And dug the knife in as 'twere a butcher.   85

I value loyalty and fealty;
Both in short supply when it comes to thee.
Thou wast justice secretary; now thou
Art poetic justice secretary.

GOVE   'Tis the best one yet, Prime Minister.   90

MAY   I have to make room for some new faces.
In my cabinet thou now hast no place.
In the words of Lord Sugar: 'Thou art fir'd.'

GOVE   Thankyoufortheopportunity, as
They say ev'ry time on *The Apprentice*.   95
The stubby finger of doom is raised high
And into the wilderness I am cast.
Naught except a battle lost can be half
So melancholy as a battle won.
Reputation – a false imposition,   100
Got without merit, lost without deserving.
Good name in man and woman, dear my lord,
Is the immediate jewel of their souls:
Who steals my purse steals trash; 'tis something,
     nothing;
'Twas mine, 'tis his, and has been slave to
     thousands;   105
But he that filches from me my good name,
Robs me of that which not enriches him,
And makes me poor indeed.

MAY   Why art thou still here?

                                                    [Exit Gove.

MAY   Thou hast nothing to smirk about, for sure.   110
             Thou art also fir'd.

OSBORNE   Who comes in my place?

MAY   Philip Hammond. 'Tis an excellent name.
             That of my husband, and of the Queen's too.
             [*Aside:*] They are not the same Philip, obviously.   115
             Mine can be trust'd to get through the day
             Without saying something mildly racist.

OSBORNE   Spreadsheet Phil? Old Box Office Hammond himself?

MAY   Now 'tis not the time for pyrotechnics.
             Now we need a steady hand at the helm.   120
             Pray leave thy ministerial car here.
             Thou canst take an Addison Lee cab home.

                                                    [Exit Osborne.

MAY   [*To Fox, Davis and Johnson:*] Now, the three Brexiteers,
                 though I do fear
             That 'tis less one for all and all for one;
             And instead, ev'ry man out for himself.   125
             Liam, thou art International Trade;
             David, thou heads the Brexit department;
             And Boris, thou art Foreign Secretary.

JOHNSON   'Tis the strangest move in politics since

                Caligula made his horse senator.   130

MAY   Let none say I have no sense of humour.

                The least diplomatic man sent abroad

                To charm and represent our great nation.

                I confess: when the idea came to me,

                My laughter was so long and most ribald,   135

                I truly thought my pants would never dry.

                The more I can have thee in foreign climes,

                The less harm canst thou cause on these fair shores.

                There is method in my madness, for sure.

                                                        [Exeunt.

SCENE 8

A room in Brussels.

Enter JEAN-CLAUDE JUNCKER, DONALD TUSK
and MICHEL BARNIER.

JUNCKER   Double, double, toil and trouble;

                Fire burn, and cauldron bubble!

TUSK   By the pricking of my thumbs,

                Something Brexit this way comes.

BARNIER   When shall we three meet again   5

In Brussels, Strasbourg, or Berlin?
When the hurly-burly's done?
When the battle's lost and won?

JUNCKER   When the first bottle's open'd and pour'd?

TUSK   'Tis meet and right to meet right now;   10
           'Twill be but the first of many.
           Brexit means Brexit, so Theresa says;
           But Brexit comes in at least four flavours.

BARNIER   First, soft Brexit: soft as the satin fringe
           That shades the eyelids of thy fragrant maids.   15
           Soft as foot can fall, soft as marshmallow;
           Soft as showers that sprinkle April meads.
           Soft as the evening wind amongst willows,
           Soft as the sand trod by dainty seraphs.
           Soft as morning sun, soft as zephyr's wing.   20
           Soft as the gentle breathing of the lute;
           Soft as the melody of youthful days.
           Soft as the cooing of the turtle dove.
           Soft as Naples silk, soft as Lempster wool.
           Soft as the whisper shut within a shell.   25

TUSK   Fie, Barnier! Dost thou intend to win
           The negotiations by boring them?

BARNIER   Thou Polish philistine! I, a Frenchman,
           Must wax lyrical; 'tis my nation's right.

A soft Brexit, aye. Customs union   30
And single market are both for Britain;
They must accept rules and regulations,
And continue budget contributions.

JUNCKER   Next, Norway. 'Tis in the single market
But 'tis not in the customs union.   35
[*Aside:*] 'Tis too a member of the EEA
(EU countries, Liechtenstein and Iceland);
And EFTA (plus Switzerland, Liechtenstein
And Iceland again, but not the EU).
Needlessly complex? Why, this is Europe.   40

TUSK   Third, Canada. A bespoke trade deal sign'd;
Though with Canada seven years this did take.
No budget contributions, ECJ
Or four freedoms do they need to accept.

BARNIER   Last, and let us pray least, a hard Brexit.   45
All bar declaring war on Germany.

JUNCKER   They will be pro-cake and pro-eating it.
We must restrict their access to all cakes
Originating in the EU, no?
No aranygaluska, no babka;   50
No baumkuchen, bienenstich, blitz torte;
Buccellato, cassata, cremeschnitte;
Croquembouche, dacquoise, eierschecke, garash;
Genoise, joffre, karpatka, kladdkaka;

Kolaczki, kransekake, kremowka;   55

Makowiec, magdalena, mille-feuille;

Ostkaka, panettone, petits fours;

Prinzregententorte, punschkrapfen, sponge;

Streuselkuchen, tatin nor tiramisu.

TUSK   Your knowledge of EU wines I did know;   60

But cakes too, thou art verily expert.

JUNCKER   I am a man of many talents. Come!

'Tis opening time, and I have a thirst.

[Exeunt.

SCENE 9

Enter KUENSSBERG *with a cameraman.*

KUENSSBERG   To the High Court, for R (Miller) versus

Secretary of State for Exiting the

European Union [*Aside:*] A catchy title.

Yes, said the judges, Parliament must pass

Legislation for Article 50.   5

Foul! cri'd Eurosceptics and Brexiteers.

Enemies of the People! shriek'd the *Mail*;

As Robespierre did once shriek; Lenin, too.

To Washington, and the triumph of Trump;

Shaking hands with his new bestie Nigel   10

In a gold-plat'd elevator.

'Was my election bigger than Brexit?'

'Your election was Brexit plus plus plus.'

Nigel as ambassador in DC?

He'd do a great job, according to Trump.   15

Not on your nelly, said the government.

Then to Lancaster House, and a 'clean break'.

Theresa laid out her plans for Brexit;

Leave the single market, and abandon

Full membership of t'customs union.   20

A new partnership: not half-in, half-out.

Comprehensive, and bold, and ambitious,

And 'no deal is better than a bad deal'.

Finally, 29th March 2017.

Major's birthday, Blair's anniversary;   25

And the day May signed Article 50.

Two years to leave from now; the clock running.

Now back to you in the studio, Huw.

[Exit Kuenssberg.

ACT III

SCENE 1

The anteroom to the Prime Minister's office, 10 Downing Street.

Enter NICK TIMOTHY, *balding with a lustrous beard like
some 19th-century Russian poet, and* FIONA HILL,
a livewire Scot with ginger hair.

HILL   He's Nick Timothy.

TIMOTHY   She's Fiona Hill.

HILL   We are the Rosencrantz and Guildenstern
                  To Theresa May's Princess Hamlet.
                  Nothing gets to the PM, or past her,   5
                  Without going through us in the first place.

TIMOTHY   They call us the chiefs, keepers of the gate;
                  Theresa trusts us both implicitly;
                  Upon our loyal advice she depends.
                  She takes no big decision without us.   10

HILL   No small one, either, if the truth be told.
                  The children she could not bear? 'Tis for Freud,
                  That way of thought, but some truth there may be.
                  She ignores our flaws as we ignore hers.

TIMOTHY   We stand ready in the night against those   15
            Who would do her harm, and they are legion.
            She pledg'd to end the sofa government,
            And aye, she has done so; 'tis now three chairs.

HILL   People call us siblings: we fight a lot.
            Free, frank and oft times brutally honest.   20
            Don't care what we say about the other.
            But united we always stand in public.

TIMOTHY   No cigarette paper comes between us
            To the outside world. She covers my arse,
            And I cover hers. No divide and rule.   25
            No one can ever split us asunder.

HILL   We are not popular, and we don't care.
            We are Theresa, and she too is us.
            Some cabinet ministers despise us;
            Officials and civil servants, they too.   30

TIMOTHY   We collect scalps like ancient headhunters;
            For many enemies adorn a man.
            The terrible twins, the gruesome twosome;
            Such monikers to us are pride, not shame.

HILL   *Oderint dum metuant*; let them hate   35
            So long as they fear. And fear they must do.
            Here, Waiting Room B, the Bollocking Room,
            We tear strips off thee as though by blowtorch.

TIMOTHY   With beard and power, I am Rasputin.

HILL   But not Downing Street's greatest love machine.   40

TIMOTHY   'Tis a shame, Fiona, how you carry on.
               Thou art a feline who really has gone.

HILL   I am volatile, perchance quicksilver;
               A tiger's mouth canst snap shut any time.
               Fie, look sharp! Here comes Theresa, the boss.   45

TIMOTHY   *We* are the bosses.

HILL   Aye, but we must let her think that she is.

TIMOTHY   'Tis true.

                    Enter THERESA MAY.

MAY   Rosencrantz, Guildenstern, fine day.

HILL   'Tis fine if it involves the following: 50
               Crushing our enemies, and seeing them
               Driven before us, and of course hearing
               The lamentation of all the women.

MAY   Funny thou shouldst say that. Philip and I
               Have just been walking in Snowdonia.   55
               Have you been? 'Tis the most beautiful place.

While we were there I did purchase a book.
Here… *Walks In And Around Dolgellau Town.*
Let me read some to you. 'During the walk,
There are a series of revelations.   60
Moments of discovery: mind-cleansing.
They give you that moment of clarity
To help make those important decisions.'

HILL   Let me see…

HILL *takes the book and glances at the cover.*

HILL   The author, Michael Burnett;   65
              Truly, the Buddha of Snowdonia.

TIMOTHY   What cleansing revelation hast thou had?

HILL   No decision. Not without calling us.

MAY   Philip and I think it a good idea—

TIMOTHY   [*Together:*] We'll be the judge of that—   70
and HILL

MAY   —To take a chance.
              Carpe the *diem*, secure a mandate.

TIMOTHY   Call an election?

HILL   Go to the country?

MAY *nods.* TIMOTHY *and* HILL *confer sotto voce.*

HILL   [*Aside:*] Good idea. We're glad you agree with us.   75
                                              [*Exeunt.*

SCENE 2

Enter KUENSSBERG *with a cameraman.*

KUENSSBERG There were those who caution'd agin this course.
            She had promis'd no sudden election,
            She had a workable majority;
            Why twist when she could just keep on sticking?
            Why risk an advantage, e'en a small one?   5
            More, though, who thought her most brave and most
                right.
            They recall'd Gordon Brown (texture like sun)
            Who had vacillat'd, hesitat'd,
            Eventually decid'd not to run;
            Never won a vote as Prime Minister.   10
            All omens did seem good for the Tories;
            Twenty points up on Labour in the polls,
            Theresa's personal ratings superb.
            Vict'ry in the Copeland by-election,
            A government's first for thirty-five years.   15
            She told the Cabinet, who laud'd her.

'This is exactly why you're the right person
to lead us, Prime Minister.' The words of
Justine Greening, Order of the Brown Nose.
A reluctant leader, to the public;   20
Substance of unflashy steely resolve.
Half John Major's warm village cricket beer,
Half Maggie's unbending, unturning steel.
Or the cult of no personality?
Not everyone was pleas'd, needless to say;   25
Over to Brenda in Bristol, vox popp'd.

BRENDA   [*Within:*] You're joking? Not another election?
                Oh, for God's sake! I can't stand this. There's too
                Much politics going on at the moment.
                Why does she need to do it?   30

KUENSSBERG   Brenda there.
             And then it all began to unravel.
             The so-called dementia tax, under which
             Anyone with capital and income
             Above twenty-three thousand pounds   35
             Had to pay their own residential care.
             Sell their homes to pay for it? If need be.
             This didn't play badly, but terribly.
             Sailing serenely along, and then crashing
             Into an iceberg of their own making.   40

                                       [*Exit Kuenssberg.*

             Enter MAY *out on the campaign trail.*

MAY   We have plac'd a cap on contributions.

             I've been very, very clear. Nothing has chang'd.

             The manifesto principles are sound.

                 Her voice rises higher and cracks a little.

             Our government must be strong and stable.

             Strong and stable. Stable and strong. Must be.   45

             Strong, like Mark Strong the actor, tall and bald;

             Stable, whose door you shut after the horse

             Has bolted more quickly than Usain Bolt.

             Her eyes flash with a combination of fury and fear.

             I've been very, very clear. I am the Maybot.

             Well-programm'd, aye, but prone to malfunction.   55

             Whirr. Clunk. Clang. I take some time to warm up.

         Now she's in an ITV studio with JULIE ETCHINGHAM.

ETCHINGHAM What's the naughtiest thing you've ever done?

MAY   Oh goodness me. Well… but I suppose the…

             Nobody's ever perfectly behaved,

             Are they? When my friends and I used to run   60

             Through the fields of wheat, the farmers weren't too

                 pleased.

                                                     [Exeunt.

Enter KUENSSBERG *with a cameraman.*

KUENSSBERG   Meanwhile, Jeremy Corbyn was uniting
              Lenin and Lennon, Bolshevik and Beatle.
              The hard left seeking proper socialism,
              The young idealists, all urgent and keen.   65

Enter CORBYN, *on stage at Glastonbury, in front of a* CROWD.

CROWD   [*Within:*] Ooooh, Je-rem-eee Corrr-byn; Ooooh,
                  Je-rem-eee
              Corrr-byn, Ooooh, Je-rem-eee Corrr-byn…
                                                          [*Exit crowd.*

Enter MAY.

MAY   Jeremy Corbyn calls Hamas 'our friends'.
              He will not get a sole majority.
              You get a coalition of chaos   70
              Propped up by pretty extreme radicals.

KUENSSBERG   And gradually the gap began to close.
              Now back to you in the studio, Huw.
                                                          [*Exeunt.*

SCENE 3

THERESA MAY's *constituency house, Maidenhead. Election night.*

Enter TIMOTHY, HILL, MAY *and her husband,* PHILIP.

DAVID DIMBLEBY *appears on TV.*

TIMOTHY	We've had no time to plan for government.
	This campaign has exhausted all of us.

HILL	Aye, but 'twill be worth it when we win big.
	A majority of 50 seats, say.

DIMBLEBY	[*Within:*] 'Tis ten o'clock. We have the exit polls.	5
	Britain is facing a hung parliament.	
	Theresa May's gamble looks to have failed.	
	She sought certainty and stability;	
	And has found neither one nor the other.	
	Now over to Professor John Curtice,	10
	The Santa Claus of opinion polls.	
	He's making a list, he's checking it twice;	
	He's gonna find out who's won Haltemprice.	

A long pause.

TIMOTHY	They must have got it wrong. This is not right.

HILL	Nay, 'tis right. Exit polls usually are.	15

MAY *begins to weep softly.* PHILIP *gives her a hug.*

OSBORNE *appears on TV, clearly relishing the moment.*

OSBORNE	[*Within:*] The worst thing Theresa's done in her life
	Is no longer running through a wheat field.

DIMBLEBY	[*Within:*] Art thou tempted to run for Parliament?

OSBORNE	[*Within:*] For the seat of Schadenfreude Central.

TIMOTHY   I shall shave off my beard and go into   20
           A witness protection programme.

HILL   Witless,
           More like. How could we have got it so wrong?
                                                    [Exeunt.

SCENE 4

The election count in Maidenhead.

Enter THERESA MAY, *her opponent* LORD BUCKETHEAD, *a*
RETURNING OFFICER, *and* NICK TIMOTHY *and* FIONA HILL.

The candidates are on stage stood in front of a small CROWD.

RETURNING   Lord Buckethead, Independent. Votes cast:
OFFICER   Two hundred and forty-nine.

           LORD BUCKETHEAD *steps forward.*
           He has a large black bucket on his head.

LORD   I have run
BUCKETHEAD
              On a platform of leadership which is

              Strong but not entirely stable. Also,   5

              I wish that we nationalise Adele,

              Blast misbehaving kids into deep space,

              And have a referendum on whether

              We should have another referendum.

              Cheers and applause from the CROWD.

HILL   [*To Timothy:*] Some of those policies are interesting.   10

TIMOTHY   [*To Hill:*] We should incorporate them into ours.

       MAY *steps off stage and goes into a huddle with them.*

MAY   Should I go on?

TIMOTHY   Aye, you must. The battle is not yet won;

              And the long race is only partway run.

MAY   'Tis meet and right so to do, continue.   15

              The country needs leadership at all costs.

              The Party will demand sacrifices.

              The Cabinet may back me, at a price.

HILL   That price being our removal, I fear.

MAY   'Tis your removal or mine.   20

TIMOTHY   If you go
             We are out of Downing Street anyway.

HILL   The pawns do fall as the queen marches on.

                                              [Exeunt.

             Enter KUENSSBERG *and a cameraman.*

KUENSSBERG   The DUP backed the May government;
             A billion to Northern Ireland helped.   25
             In fairness, Theresa had warned us all
             About a coalition of chaos
             Propped up by pretty extreme radicals.
             She just forgot to say she'd be in charge.
             Further problems for her inside the tent: 30
             Boris, telling Brussels to 'go whistle'
             For the money owed in the divorce bill.
             Moggmentum rising in summer clover;
             Clamour for JRM to be PM.
             Boris again – these damned Etonians! –   35
             Speaking before the Party Conference.
             Four personal red lines have I, he said.
             Two years' transition, not a second more;
             No new ECJ rulings in that time;
             No payments for single market access;   40
             No shadowing EU rules in a deal.
             Hard deadlines where May was more flexible;
             Some direct contradictions of her plans.

Footage of JOHNSON *speaking on TV.*

JOHNSON [*Within:*] We cannot just come out of the EU,

Only to find ourselves locked in some kind   45

Of rotational orbit around it.

We and they are plainly not sun and earth,

Nor planet and satellite, tidal pulls.

Galileo I am not, nor Brahe,

Nor e'en Patrick Moore from *The Sky at Night*.   50

Brussels restaurants have made me prefer

Gastronomy over astronomy.

KUENSSBERG Once more Boris laying down the gauntlet,

Speaking of his leadership ambitions

While always denying the very same.   55

A choice for the Prime Minister sometime:

Sooner, later, either he goes or she does.

Now to Manchester, home of nineties raves

And current party conferences too.

If Theresa had considered things bad,   60

She should have remembered the wisdom of

Messrs Bachman, Turner and Overdrive.

'You ain't seen nothing yet. B-B-Boris',

Now back to you in the studio, Huw.

[Exeunt.

SCENE 5

The Conservative Party Conference.

Enter THERESA MAY *and* PHILIP HAMMOND, *who sits
alongside* MAY. *She is giving her keynote speech to A LARGE* CROWD.
*She is standing in front of a large slogan that reads: 'BUILDING
A COUNTRY THAT WORKS FOR EVERYONE.'*

BORIS JOHNSON *and* DAVID DAVIS *watch amongst the* CROWD,
alongside KUENSSBERG *and other journalists.*

MAY   The election campaign was badly run;
             'Twas too script'd. 'Twas too presidential.
             It let Labour paint us as the voice of
             Continuity, when people want change.
             I hold my hands up for that. My shoulders   5
             Bear on them the responsibility.
             I led the campaign. And I am sorry.
             Me, the unemotional ice maiden;
             Though I fear George took things a bit too far,
             When he said he want'd to chop me up,   10
             Put me in his freezer like Cap'n Birdseye.

                    The CROWD *laugh.*

MAY   'Tis great sadness for both Philip and me,
             That we two were never bless'd with children.
             It seems some things are just not meant to be.

But I believe, as much as anyone else –   15

Mother, father, grandmother, grandfather –

That life should be better for those who come

After us, for the next generation.

The only diff'rence between us is this;

I am in a privileg'd position.   20

I can do more than most to help people,

To aid them in bringing that dream to life;

In restoring hope and the British dream.

This is why I came into politics.

To make a diff'rence, change things for better,   25

And hand on to the next generation

A stronger, fairer, prosperous country.

Enter LEE NELSON, *a comedian. He approaches*
the podium and hands the PM a fake P45.

NELSON   [*To Theresa:*] Boris ask'd me to give you this.

Trying to maintain poise, THERESA *takes the paper and crumples it*
up. NELSON *goes over to* JOHNSON *and gives him a big thumbs up.*

NELSON   Art thou

                Satisfi'd with what I've done in your name?   30

Enter militiamen armed with muskets, who pull NELSON *away.*
                                [Exeunt Nelson and militiamen

DAVIS   That fellow is most fortunate, I say.

Had I hit him, he'd have stay'd down for good.

Did thou knowest I was in the SAS?

JOHNSON   Territorial SAS.

DAVIS   Still counts.   35

JOHNSON   Doth not.

DAVIS   Doth too.

JOHNSON   Doth not!

DAVIS   Doth doth doth DOTH!

MAY   [*To the crowd:*] It could have been worse. I could have
            picked up   40
            A paper cut, as Alan Partridge did,
            When he combin'd a business card swap with
            A firm handshake with a man from Nestlé.
            The man to whom I would wish to give a
            P45 is Jeremy Corbyn.   45

Applause from the CROWD.

MAY *begins to cough. Tries to speak. Coughs again. Makes a
croaky honk. It sounds like a punctur'd bagpipe, the meek whistle of
a dent'd piccolo. An aide hands her water, which she gulps down.
This only makes the coughing worse.*

KUENSSBERG   Nine pages hath she left to go through coughs.

'Tis like a nightmare. Any moment now,

She will wake up, turn to Philip, and say:

'Thou will never believe the dream I've had.'

The CROWD *rise to their feet to give* MAY *an ovation to buy her time.*
PHILIP HAMMOND *passes her a cough sweet. She takes it.*

MAY   Take note of this historic moment; 'tis   50

The Chancellor, giving something for free.

More laughter. She continues to speak through coughs which
force her to judder to a halt now and then, and make
her sound even more robotic than usual.

MAY   Why not just stop now, thou askest thyself?

'Twould be easy to cut all my losses,

And end this farce of a speech here and now.

Why not? Because I see them over there;   55

The men and women who would be ruler,

Who would take my job in an eye's blinking.

I will not give them the satisfaction.

On I go, the Maybot, replicant-like,

Like Rutger Hauer in that *Blade Runner*.   60

God rest his Guinness-drinking Dutchman's soul.

I've seen things you people wouldn't believe.

I've seen tower blocks on fire just off the

Shoulder of the White City flyover.

I've watched Angela Merkel glitt'ring   65

In the darkness near the Brandenburg Gate.
All these moments will soon be lost in time,
Like tears in rain. 'Tis time to die. Nay! Nay!
I must fight on. I live another day.

Behind her, the 'F' falls off the slogan 'BUILDING A COUNTRY
THAT WORKS FOR EVERYONE'.

KUENSSBERG   Now the 'F' is off. F off. A message?   70
She needs a stronger, more stable backdrop.
Not for the first time since Brexit, the job
Of satirist has become transcriber.
This speech cannot be call'd a mere car crash.
'Tis an enormous motorway pile-up;   75
A turd immune to spin-doctor polish.
Now back to you in the studio, Huw.

[Exeunt.

ACT IV

SCENE 1

Chequers, the country residence of the Prime Minister.

Enter KUENSSBERG *with a cameraman.*

KUENSSBERG The legal niceties are enshrin'd; the
European Union (Withdrawal)
Act 2018 repeals previous law,
Particularly the European
Communities Act 1972.   5
Guys, thou need to get some snappier names.
The new act hath several provisions;
It fixeth the exit day, formally
Incorporates pieces of EU law
While ending the supremacy of same;   10
And requires that Parliament doth approve
The outcome of the negotiations.
On the link we have Michel Barnier.
Monsieur Barnier, qu'est-ce qui se passe?

BARNIER [*Within:*] Eighty per cent of the deal is complete.   15
We want to accept a trade agreement
If it does not harm the single market.
The single market is not and should not
Be seen as a giant supermarket.
It is economic life, cultural   20

Life, and social life: all these dimensions.

KUENSSBERG   Merci. Au revoir. Behind me you can see
Members of the Cabinet arriving.
They're here to discuss Theresa's new plan,
Which she will then take along to Brussels.   25
Now back to you in the studio, Huw.

[Exit Kuenssberg.

Enter THERESA MAY *with her cabinet, including* JOHNSON.

MAY   Put your mobile phones inside this bag, please.
All of you. And all they phones. Mr Johnson,
Thou art hiding a spare in thy sock.

JOHNSON *resignedly brings out his spare mobile and
puts it in the bag too.*

I can take no risks. This place has more leaks   30
Than a colander in the middle of Wales.
Please don't blame me, I don't write my own jokes.
We will be here until we agree a course.
And no bunking off to watch Wimbledon.
But afore we start, know thee all this thing: 35
I could be well moved if I were as you.
If I could pray to move, prayers would move me.
But I am constant as the Northern Star,
Of whose true-fix'd and resting quality
There is no fellow in the firmament.   40

The skies are painted with unnumbered sparks;

They are all fire, and every one doth shine;

But there's but one in all doth hold his place.

Light fades and rises again to demonstrate the passing of time.

Enter MAY and KUENSSBERG.

MAY *stands in front of a lectern, KUENSSBERG alongside her.*

MAY   The Cabinet hath reach'd an agreement

               After hours of vigorous discussion.   45

KUENSSBERG   [*Aside:*] To translate: after hours of arguing.

MAY   There was a free and frank exchange of views.

KUENSSBERG   [*Aside:*] Big shouting. Like Christmas Day *EastEnders*.

MAY   In the end, unanimity was reach'd.

KUENSSBERG   [*Aside:*] She said they couldn't have their mobiles back   50

               Until they agreed to support this plan.

MAY   The proposals I'm about to outline

               Represent a precise, responsible

               Approach to future negotiations.

KUENSSBERG   [*Aside:*] You thought Cabinet agreement was hard?   55

Wait till you hear what the EU will say.

MAY   A true independent trade policy,

Is the first of our agreements made here.

Setting our own tariffs, making new deals.

We will maintain a common rulebook for   60

All goods, including agricultural

Products, with the EU after Brexit.

We want continued harmonisation

With EU rules, avoiding border probs.

We will avoid a hard Irish border,   65

And we will therefore not need a backstop.

We can choose to diverge from EU rules,

Though, and accept all the consequences.

Plus, a joint institutional framework

To interpret UK-EU treaties.   70

In British courts here, and EU courts there.

No more ECJ oversight for us.

No more annual payments to the EU.

We will curtail free movement of people,

But set up a mobility framework   75

Allowing British citizens to travel,

And apply for study and work within

The EU, and vice versa for them.

KUENSSBERG   [*Aside:*] All this may sound good, but in principle.

In practice, 'tis a much diff'rent matter.   80

There's more fudge to be found here than in all

The chocolate fact'ries of Britain combined.

Control tariffs but continue as though
We're still part of the customs union?
Skirting o'er the questions of services,   85
Which comprise four-fifths of t'economy?
Free movement for goods, limited access
For services, capital and people?
The EU are as likely to wear this
As they are to dance a jig in a fez.   90
The big beasts will be up in arms at this.
Cry havoc, and let slip the dogs of war.
Now back to you in the studio, Huw.

[Exeunt.

SCENE 2

10 Downing Street.

Enter MAY. *She is working at her desk. There is a knock on the door.*

MAY   Come.

A FLUNKEY *enters.*

FLUNKEY   Mr Davis is here to see you, ma'am.

MAY   'Tis fine.

[Exit Flunkey.

Enter DAVID DAVIS.

MAY   To what do I owe the pleasure?

DAVIS   I am, as you know, Secretary of State   5
             For Exiting the European Union.

MAY   Of course I know. I appoint'd you.

DAVIS   Aye.
             Now I am exiting the Department
             For Exiting the European Union.   10
             This may be Brexit: I am D-Dexit.
             Alliteration, and not a stammer.

MAY   Thou hast chosen not to fight the good fight?

DAVIS   No, I hath come to the end of my tether.
             Many a time have I disagree'd with   15
             The official Number Ten policy.
             The sequencing of negotiations,
             The choice of language on Northern Ireland;
             I have accept'd these, and others too,
             Through collective responsibility.   20
             Back then I consider'd it possible
             To deliver on the Referendum,
             And the mandate it had afford'd us.
             I have always been clear—

MAY   That is my phrase.   25

               Let me be clear, you must find your own one.

DAVIS   —that we must leave the customs union

               And the single market. Properly leave.

               De facto as well as *de jure*.

MAY   Fie!   30

               'Tis like having Boris here, this Latin.

DAVIS   Our current policy and tactics trend

               Is making this less, and not more, likely.

               Our right to diverge has been dilut'd,

               The White Paper delay'd without reason,   35

               The backstop present'd without failsafe.

               Our negotiating position weak,

               Possibly catastrophically so.

               And parliament'ry control of the process

               Will be illusory rather than real.   40

               The more we give, the more they will demand.

               Maybe thou art correct and I am wrong.

               Thou need a believ'r in your approach,

               And I am no long'r the man for that.

               I am now but a reluctant conscript.   45

               'Tis not enough for either thee or me.

               Therefore I tender my resignation.

MAY   'Tis a great shame, I cannot deny that.

               We are making good progress on Brexit,

                  Consistent with the twin mandates of the   50
                  Referendum and our manifesto.
                  I believe we will take back our control.
                  But the choice is thine, and I respect it.

DAVIS   Prime Minister.

                  DAVIS turns to leave, and then turns back.

DAVIS   Après moi, le déluge.   55
                                      [Exit Davis.

                    Enter BORIS JOHNSON.

MAY   Hast thou come to resign too?

JOHNSON   Aye, for sure.
                  To sell this plan is to polish a turd.
                  Opportunity, optimism, hope:
                  Those to me are what Brexit is about.   60
                  It should let us do things differently,
                  To be more nimble and more dynamic.
                  But that dream is dying: slowly, surely,
                  Asphyxiat'd by needless self-doubt.
                  We are heading for a semi-Brexit,   65
                  Lock'd into a system we can't control.
                  Indeed, I fear we have e'en gone backwards.
                  We are head'd for colony, vassal;
                  Shorn of might, majesty and influence.

We are sending our vanguard to battle   70

With the white flags fluttering above them.

The government now has a song to sing,

But I practis'd the words on the weekend

And I find that they do stick in my throat.

I cannot in all conscience—   75

MAY   Conscience? Thee!

JOHNSON   Champion these proposals. I must go.

MAY   I – ah, repeating myself is too hard.

Ask Davis what I said to him just now.

And don't let the door hit you in the arse   80

On your way out. In the name of God, go!

JOHNSON   I note the Olly Cromwell reference.

A Puritan, like yourself, I am sure.

Some of us take pleasure more extreme than

Running through wheat fields.   85

MAY   'Tis but white noise to me.

                                              [Exeunt.

SCENE 3

A TV report.

Enter KUENNSBERG *with a cameraman.*

KUENNSBERG   Where BoJo and DD had trod, so too
               The EU follow'd. Nay, nay, and thrice nay.
               Nie, said Tusk. Non for Macron. Merkel? Nein!
               Theresa May's plans they sure reject'd.
               The single market's integrity? Total.   5
               This cannot be violat'd, said Barnier.
               'No cherry-picking of the four freedoms.'
               E'en Donald Trump weigh'd in while in Britain.
               No trade deal with the US as things stand:
               That's what he said [*Aside:*]or probably Tweet'd.   10
               'You're doing a fantastic job,' he said
               To Theresa at Chequers later on.
               The 'no trade deal' line? Fake news! Just fake news!
               Summer turn'd to autumn, and to winter.
               A final proposal May did proffer;   15
               Too much for Dominic Raab, who resign'd
               As Brexit Secretary after just four months.
               [*Aside:*] Rumour had it that his staff much liked to add
               As many 'a's to his name as they could.
               In official documents, the record   20
               Was five: 'Raaaaab'. Did he perchance drive a Saab?
               He was replac'd by Stephen Barclay. Who?
               Good question. He was not a household name
               E'en in his own household. Strange days indeed.
               Now back to you in the studio, Huw.   25

                                               [*Exeunt.*

SCENE 4

A meeting of the European Research Group.

Enter JACOB REES-MOGG, *looking like a haunt'd pencil*
in a double-breasted suit. He addresses the room.

REES-MOGG   Now is the winter of our discontent

Gone, glorious 2016 summer;

And all the clouds, that lour'd upon our house,

In the deep bosom of Parliament buried.

Now are our brows bound with Brexit problems;   5

Our bruised arms hung up for three-line whips;

Our stern alarums charg'd with covert meetings,

Our dreadful marches with purposeful measures.

Grim-visag'd war hath smooth'd our wrinkled fronts;

Boris! Instead of mounting barbed steeds,   10

To fright the souls of fearful adversaries,

He capers nimbly in a lady's chamber

To the lascivious pleasing of a lute.

But I, that am not shap'd for sportive tricks,

Nor made to court an amorous looking-glass;   15

I, that am rudely stamp'd, and want love's majesty,

To strut before a wanton ambling nymph;

I, that am curtail'd of this fair proportion,

By my faith and my full six progeny,

Nanni'd, cosset'd, sent before this time   20

To campaign in Fife, and in Manchester,

And that so lamely and unfashionable,

That dogs bark'd at me, as I stopp'd by them.

Why, I, in that weak piping time of peace,

Has no delight to pass away the time,   25

Unless to spy my Roller in the sun

And descant on mine own fine limousine.

And therefore, since I cannot prove a lover

To entertain these fair well-spoken days,

I am determined to prove a villain   30

And hate the idle pleasures of these days.

Plots have I laid, inductions dangerous,

By drunken prophecies, libels, and dreams,

To set Mrs Theresa and myself

In deadly hate the one against the other: 35

And if Theresa be as true and just

As I am subtle, false and treacherous,

This day should Boris closely be mew'd up –

About a prophecy which says that he

Of Brexit's heirs the murderer shall be.   40

Dive, thoughts, down to my soul.

Gentlemen! We have forty-eight letters.

Enough for a vote of no confidence.

E'en if some of them do not conform to

The grammar rules for which I'm a stickler.   45

Here: only one space after a full stop.

Here: a gentleman's name without 'Esquire.'

And in this epistle, author nameless

To spare their blushes, we find these bann'd words.

'No longer fit for purpose.' 'Hopefully.'   50

'Unacceptable.' 'Meet with.' 'Ascertain.'
'Ongoing.' 'Speculate.' 'Disappointment.'
This mangling of the language appals me.
Fie! At least he has not call'd me 'thyself.'
Still. The letters are in, as we require.   55
Let us put them, and ourselves, to the test.
Let us see whether the Party backs her.
She will contest, of that I have no doubt.

                                          [*Exeunt.*

SCENE 5

A Commons committee room in Westminster.

The room is packed with Conservative MPs: sitting on tables,
crouching on the floor, pinned against the windows.

Enter MAY, GOVE, GRAHAM BRADY *and* JACOB REES-MOGG.
KUENSSBERG *appears at the edge of the scene.*

MAY   Dost thou really want to change horses now?
                I know I'm not first choice for many here,
                But get rid of me, and then what happens?
                Brexit delay'd, for sure. An election?
                Corbyn in Number Ten? A disaster.   5
                The next election is due in four years.
                I pledge to thee: I will not lead us then.
                In my heart I would like to, but I see

Which way the wind is blowing here, for sure.
Let me deliver Brexit, and stand down.   10
Friends, Romans, countrymen, lend me your votes.

They begin to cast their votes in the ballot box.

GOVE   The Prime Minister will win handsomely.

KUENSSBERG   [*Aside:*] What will be her margin of victory?

GOVE   I studi'd English, not maths. I'll stick with
                Handsomely.   15

KUENSSBERG   [*Aside:*] We've had quite enough of experts, eh?

SIR GRAHAM BRADY, *Chairman of the 1922 Committee,*
takes the chair.

BRADY   Prithee, silence! The results are now in.
                Votes for the Prime Minister: two hundred.
                Votes agin: one hundred and seventeen.
                No further confidence vote can be held   20
                For at least one year under standing rules.

REES-MOGG   The Prime Minister has lost the support
                Of a third of her MPs. Resign? Yes.
                She has diligence and stamina, but
                Stamina is no kind of strategy.   25
                Can'st thou, O partial sleep! give thy repose

To the wet sea-boy in an hour so rude;

And, in the calmest and most stillest night,

With all appliances and means to boot,

Deny it to a queen? Then, happy low, lie down!   30

Uneasy lies the head that wears a crown.

SCENE 6

The House of Commons chamber, January 2019.

MPs on both sides are debating. Enter MR SPEAKER, *Speaker of the House of Commons and a voluble gnome-like figure,* GEOFFREY COX, DOMINIC RAAB, KENNETH CLARKE, SAMMY WILSON, MICHAEL GOVE, JEREMY CORBYN *and* THERESA MAY.

MR SPEAKER   Geoffrey Cox, the Attorney General.

COX   Two choices lie before us on this day;

             Accept the deal, or there's no-deal chaos.

             We are legislators, each one of us,

             To contemplate with equanimity   5

             This situation; 'twould be the very

             Summit of irresponsibility.

             Imagine the members of the public.

             Imagine what they will say, and rightly.

             'What are you playing at? What are you doing?   10

             You are not children in the playground.

             You are legislators. This is your job.'

MR SPEAKER   Dominic Raab.

RAAB   Thank you, Mr Speaker.
         I have always tried hard to understand   15
         The case for compromise, but compromise
         Cannot come at any price, least this deal.
         'Tis the most severe and enduring risk
         For economy and democracy.
         'Tis so demeaning that 'twould sure invite –   20
         Nay, not invite. Demand! 'Twould sure demand –
         Reversal the moment the ink was dry.

MR SPEAKER   Mr Ken Clarke.

CLARKE   Thank you, Mr Speaker.
           For my friends who are hard-line Brexiteers,   25
           The cause seems increasingly now to be
           A religiously binding commitment.

MR SPEAKER   Mr Sammy Wilson, spokesman for the
               Democratic Unionist Party.

WILSON   My people fought a terrorist campaign   30
           To stay part of the United Kingdom.
           We will not permit Brussels bureaucrats
           To cleave us from the United Kingdom.

MR SPEAKER   Michael Gove, Environment Secretary.

GOVE   Is the House now au fait with *Game of Thrones*?   35

                'Tis a TV drama, most popular.

                Sociopathic rulers feud, squabble,

                And wreak havoc on their Brit-like country.

                All similarities to real people

                Are entirely coincidental, natch.   40

                And if we don't vote for the deal tonight

                Then winter is coming, to quote Jon Snow.

                [*Aside:*] Ned Stark's son, not the TV newsreader

                With a nice line in colourful neckties.

                This deal is the door through which we can walk;   45

                Leave the EU, determine our future.

MR SPEAKER   The Right Honourable Jeremy Corbyn.

CORBYN   The Prime Minister has treat'd Brexit

                As a matter for the Tory Party,

                And not the good of the country entire.   50

                Her efforts to steer this through Parliament

                Have been chaotic, extraordinary.

                Thirty-five years have I been a member;

                Never have I seen such a fiasco.

                This deal is a reckless leap in the dark.   55

                Two years from now we will face a stark choice:

                Pay more, extend the transition period;

                Or be lock'd forever in the backstop.

                The EU'd have us over a barrel,

                By the short and curlies, where they want us.   60

                No rebate, but liable still to pay;

Or a backstop without limit or end.

MR SPEAKER   The Prime Minister, Theresa May.

MAY   'Tis the most significant vote which we,

              All of us, will surely ever undertake.   65

              Debate and division are past. 'Tis time

              To make a decision for years to come.

              To show the people their voices are heard,

              That their trust in us has not been misplac'd.

The Division Bell sounds. The MPs file through their respective lobbies
and are counted by the clerks, who hand their tallies to the Speaker.

MR SPEAKER   Ayes to the right, two hundred and two.   70

              Noes to the left, four hundred and thirty-two.

              The noes have it! The noes have it! Unlock.

MAY   The House has spoken and we will listen.

                                                    [Exeunt.

KUENSSBERG   The largest government defeat ever;

              The margin greater than worst predictions.   75

              The vote was delay'd since before Christmas.

              To win over waverers. Ha! Fat chance!

              Party lines torn asunder. One hundred

              And eighteen Tories voting to reject.

              A piece of history, though unwant'd.   80

              Enemies uniting agin her deal;

They agree only on what they don't want.

Harder? Softer? Just anything but this.

'Tis hard to see where she goes from this place;

Caught betwixt both Brussels and Westminster.　　85

For May, 'tis a true nightmare without end.

She paint'd herself into a corner,

With her red lines so early: commitments

To leave the single market, ECJ

And customs union. No hard border　　90

'Tween Northern Ireland and the Republic.

Her choice, taken freely: placate the right.

Paint Britain as a global Gulliver

Bound by European Lilliputians.

Give the Eurosceptics what they want'd.　　95

But they prov'd never to be satisfi'd.

Now back to you in the studio, Huw.

　　　　　　　　　　　　[Exit Kuenssberg.

SCENE 7

10 Downing Street.

Enter THERESA MAY *and her husband,* PHILIP.

PHILIP　　　　Look, you have such a February face;

　　　　　　So full of frost, of storm and cloudiness.

THERESA　　　'Tis no surprise. I do aught but argue;

With Barnier, Juncker, Macron, Merkel;

Corbyn, Johnson, Rees-Mogg, Davis, and more.   5

All lin'd agin me. I have of late – but

Wherefore I know not – lost all my mirth, forgone all

Custom of exercises; and indeed it goes so heavily

With my disposition that this goodly frame, the

Earth, seems to me a sterile promontory, this most   10

Excellent canopy, the air, look you, this brave

O'erhanging firmament, this majestical roof fretted

With golden fire, why, it appears no other thing to

Me than a foul and pestilent congregation of vapours.

What a piece of work is a man! How noble in reason!   15

How infinite in faculty! In form and moving how

Express and admirable! In action how like an angel!

In apprehension how like a god! The beauty of the

World! The paragon of animals! And yet, to me,

What is this quintessence of dust?   20

PHILIP   Don't know,
           Old girl. But chin up. As the Latin goes:
           Illegitimi non carborundum.

                                                  [Exeunt.

SCENE 8

Enter KUENSSBERG *with a cameraman.*

KUENSSBERG   Back and forth she went, winter turn'd to spring.

Second vote on the Withdrawal Agreement,

And a second heavy, bruising defeat.

The House then vot'd agin a no deal.

No chance of leaving on March 29th;   5

To Brussels, begging for an extension.

A complex menu of EU options;

Dates for a new plan, or a longer time.

To Chequers again, some Tory MPs.

There would be lunch. Given the divisions,   10

It would feel as if Hannibal Lecter –

Doctor, polymath, serial killer –

Was serving them their own well-sautéed brains.

Rumour had it there would be thirteen at table.

Like the Last Supper, and that turned out well.   15

Here, Iain Duncan Smith in his Morgan.

Sporting baseball cap and sheepskin gilet.

Oi! Iain! The golf course is over there.

Here, Jacob Rees-Mogg, with one of his sons.

The one who looks and dresses just like him.   20

What would the child be doing all day long?

Bor'd rigid while the grown-ups spoke Brexit.

Should be on Fortnite, or nicking hubcaps.

Or reading the *FT*, as his father

Was doing at around about the same age.   25

The Withdrawal Agreement, third time round;

And third time defeat'd, tho 'twas closer.

Eight indicative votes in the Commons.

No deal? Standstill agreement? Permanent

Customs union? Revoke Article   30

50? Common Market 2.0?

Second Referendum? Alternative

Labour plan? Or EFTA and EEA

Membership? Majority came there none,

Not for any of them, not even one.   35

Exit day come and gone, into April;

The cruellest month, as Eliot once said.

(Thomas Stearns, aye, not the kid from *E.T.*)

Talks between Labour and Conservative;

A charade, doom'd to fail from the outset.   40

The EU offering an extension;

To Hallowe'en, strictly no longer.

Take part in European elections;

That, too, was a firm condition for May.

[*Aside:*]Both the month and the Prime Minister, aye. 45

Those elections weren't bad for Theresa;

They were disastrous. Nigel Farage, back,

Leading the Brexit Party, hoov'ring votes.

A new party winning twenty-nine seats.

A Liberal Democrat resurgence,   50

[*Aside:*] There's a sentence I thought I'd never say;

Gaining fifteen seats, Bollocks to Brexit.

[*Aside:*] 'Twas their slogan; snappy, and it sure work'd.

Conservative Party? Decimat'd.

They lost fifteen seats, keeping only four.   55

For Theresa, 'twas surely the last straw.

Now back to you in the studio, Huw.

                                                    [*Exeunt.*

SCENE 9

An anteroom of the Prime Minister's office.

Enter BRADY, *who sits down.*

BRADY   If it were done when 'tis done, then 'twere well

It were done quickly; if the assassination

Could trammel up the consequence, and catch,

With this surcease success; that but this blow

Might be the be-all and the end-all here,   5

But here, upon this bank and shoal of time,

We'd jump the life to come.

Enter FLUNKEY.

FLUNKEY   Prime Minister

May will see you now, Sir Graham.

BRADY   Thank you.   10

BRADY goes in. The lights dim. We see two silhouettes in shadow,
talking earnestly. When the lights come up, MAY is standing
at a lectern outside the famous black door.

MAY   Since I first stepp'd through the door behind me

As Prime Minister, I have striven to

Make this country work well for everyone,

And honour the Referendum result.
I feel as certain today as I did   15
Three years ago; in a democracy,
If you give people a choice, you have a
Duty to implement what they decide.
I have done my best to do that. I have
Negotiat'd the terms of our exit   20
And a new relationship with Europe
That protects jobs, our security, and
Our union. I have done everything
I can to convince MPs that they should
Back that deal. But I have not manag'd it.   25
I tried three times. 'Twas right to persevere,
Even when the odds were sore agin success.
'Tis now clear to me that 'tis for the best
That a new Prime Minister takes this on.
I will resign on the seventh of June.   30
The process of finding my successor
Will begin during the week after that.
'Tis, and shall always be, a matter of
Deep regret that I have not been able
To deliver Brexit. 'Twill be for my   35
Successor to seek a way forward that
Honours the Referendum result.
They will have to secure consensus in
Parliament where I have not, and this needs
Those on all sides of the debate to be   40
Willing to compromise. 'Twould be a first.
Compromise is not a dirty word, nay.
In other words: the best of luck, Boris.

Thou shalt soon find that 'tis not as easy

As it looks from the outside; not at all.   45

This country is a union. Not just

A family of four nations, but a

Union of people – each one of us.

Our politics may be under strain, aye,

But there is much good about this country.   50

This job has been the honour of my life.

I leave with no ill will. If you believe

That, you'll believe anything. Enormous

And enduring is my gratitude to

Have had the opportunity to serve   55

The country I love.

Her voice cracks with emotion.

And now 'tis over.

How weary, stale, flat, and unprofitable

Seem to me all the uses of this world.

Men at some time are masters of their fates: 60

The fault, dear Philip, is not in our stars,

But in ourselves, that we are underlings.

What else to say? O, I go, Brexiteers;

The potent poison quite o'er-crows my spirit:

I cannot stay to hear the news from Europe;   65

But I do prophesy the election lights

On – I won't say who has my dying voice;

So tell them, with the occurrents, more and less,

Which have solicited. The rest is silence.

                                        [Exeunt.

ACT V

SCENE 1

Enter KUENSSBERG *with a cameraman.*

KUENSSBERG   They come to bury Theresa, not to praise her.

The evil that men do lives after them;

The good is oft interr'd with their bones;

So let it be with Theresa. The noble Boris

Hath told you Theresa was ambitious: 5

If it were so, it was a grievous fault;

And grievously hath Theresa answer'd it.

Here, under leave of Govey and the rest,

For J. Hunt is an honourable man;

So are they all, all honourable men,   10

Come they to speak at Theresa's funeral.

And then stake their claims to the job she had.

Three hundred and thirteen Tory MPs

Shall whittle the candidates down to two;

One hundred and sixty thousand members   15

Of the Conservative Party shall choose.

From those two a victor shall true emerge.

Like Achilles' triumph over Hector

[*Aside:*] Though hopefully without the aftermath;

No corpse being dragg'd by no chariot.   20

So, who puts themselves up for the top job?

'Tis like that film, *Avengers Assemble*,

Though without any superheroes.

Candidates Assemble, perchance. The Dirty

Dozen, not-so-Magnificent Seven.   25

[*Aside:*] At least once a few have fallen away.

Without further ado – of that there has

Already been far too much – here they are.

The runners and riders, in their own words.

Alphabetical order, 'tis most fair.   30

                                   [Exit Kuenssberg.

Enter GOVE, HANCOCK, HARPER, HUNT, JAVID,
JOHNSON, LEADSOM, M^CVEY, RAAB *and* STEWART.
They appear as though they are contestants on a game show.

GOVE   You know me, the Iago of last time.

Back once again with the ill behaviour.

They do call me the Renegade Master.

Three ministries have I been in charge of –

Education, justice, environment –   35

And in each I have been a true zealot,

More reformer than a Pilates bed.

I led from the front in the Leave campaign.

I desire a full stop to the backstop.

If you want to stop Boris, I'm your man.   40

The truth is that you could do worse than me;

The fear's that you almost certainly will.

HANCOCK   I'm Matt Hancock, third most famous Hancock.

Ahead of me are Tony and Herbie.

Tony and his half hour: rest assur'd that   45

I won't keep you as long. That's an armful!

'Twas funnier when he said it, I know.

Herbie, jazz musician extraordinaire.

'Cantaloupe Island', 'Watermelon Man';

Other tracks using fruits in the title.   50

And eighties single 'Rockit' too, of course.

These apart, no Hancocks stand above me.

Oh, hold on. There's Sheila, and that guy Nick,

Who once front'd *They Think It's All Over*.

And Will Smith's character in, er, *Hancock*.   55

They're all a bit more famous than me too.

Sixth best-known Hancock, that's me, sure as sure.

My campaign is about a front story:

A look to the future, not to the past.

This contest is true 1840s-style;   60

People banging on about the Corn Laws,

When the Industrial Revolution

Was already changing the lives of all.

I want to lower taxes, and raise the

National living wage to ten pounds an hour.   65

HARPER   I'm Mark Harper. Heard of me? No? Thought not.

HUNT   I'm an entrepreneur. I built my own

Business, and negotiate like a fiend.

'Tis now the first time I mention these things;

'Twill emphatically not be the last.   70

Me, entrepreneur. Entrepreneur, me.

I am serious and experienc'd;

A sensible man for these troubl'd times.

With Boris at the wheel, this country would

Be a clown car. With me, 'twould be a car   75

Of gravity, seriousness, intent.

Nothing flash, of course. A Ford Mondeo,

A Vauxhall Insignia, a Lexus.

('The Japanese Mercedes,' said Partridge.)

My wife is Japanese. No! She's Chinese.   80

Memo to FCO staff: bring an atlas.

JAVID   Jeremy Hunt's dad was an admiral.

My father? Well, he was a bus driver.

I grew up on the worst road in Britain

[*Aside:*] Bristol's Stapleton Road, not the A12.   85

I am Home Secretary, like Theresa

Was before she became Prime Minister.

You know, let's leave that comparison there.

JOHNSON   Once more unto the breach, dear friends, once more;

Or close the wall up with our English dead!   90

In peace, there's nothing so becomes a man,

As modest stillness and humility:

But when the blast of war blows in our ears,

Then imitate the action of the tiger;

Stiffen the sinews, summon up the blood.   95

I see you stand like greyhounds in the slips,

Straining upon the start. The game's afoot;

Follow your spirit: and upon this charge,

Cry God for Bozza! England and Saint George!

LEADSOM   Like Govey, I'm back again. Not quite sure   100

How I made it to the last two last time.

It won't happen again, thou can be sure.

McVEY   Work and pensions secretary ere I was.

Before that, GMTV presenter.

Ask Lorraine Kelly. There's no love lost there.   105

Like Dom, I am an ultra-Brexiteer,

Though my black belts are all Donna Karan.

I will bypass Parliament if need be,

Stop bringing things to the floor of the House.

RAAB   I'm a black belt in karate, thou knowest.   110

Wax on, wax off, and Mr Miyagi.

I will be tougher than anyone else.

In all these Brexit negotiations

We have been most sore humiliat'd.

Divid'd at home and demean'd abroad.   115

But no more! I will redress the balance.

No deal, if that's what it takes, at all costs.

I am prepar'd to prorogue Parliament,

As Charles the First did. But, unlike him, I

Will for sure not shiver on the scaffold.   120

Perchance invade Brussels myself, solo;

Commando in the righteous Brexit cause.

Challenging Juncker and Tusk to a bout.

Choku zuki! Haito Uchi! Keito!

Hiza geri! Tobi mikazuki!   125

Those are just my basic karate moves.

Only Putin could take me on, thou knowest.

Actually, I think judo's more his bag.

Scrap that. I'm karate man, unconquer'd.

STEWART   An Old Etonian am I, thou knowest.   130

Hast thou not had enough of our sort yet?

From diff'rent cloth am I cut, you will find.

Neither Cameron's smooth born-to-rule shtick,

Nor Boris's chaotic buffoon act.

I have been a diplomat – not a spy;   135

A regional governor in Iraq,

A Harvard professor and an author.

More: across Afghanistan have I walk'd.

They call'd me Florence of Belgravia.

Or perchance I am indeed like others.   140

Once, ask'd in the House about declining

Numbers of rural hedgehogs, I repli'd:

'*Multa novit vulpes verum echinus*

unum magnum' afore referencing

Ancient Sumerian waxen seals,   145

The prows of long-vanish'd Egyptian ships

And many Romany cures for baldness.

My real name is Roderick and not Rory.

Rod Stewart, I. Dost thou think I'm sexy?

[*Aside:*] Gordon Brown's real first name is James:

    James Brown.   150

And Theresa May's real name is Brian.

I will tell thee the truth: this will be hard.

There are no easy answers; I offer none.

No deal? That's a no from me. No no deal.

A double negative, grammarians.   155

Whatever the solution, Parliament

Must be involv'd; that is the only way.

                                                    [Exeunt.

SCENE 2

A street, somewhere in Britain.

Enter RORY STEWART, *filming himself on his smartphone.*

STEWART   Roll up, roll up, and meet the candidate!

I, Rory Stewart, meeting the people.

Come chat, come challenge, come one and come all.

I'll talk to anyone about anything.

Here I am in Barking – the joke is clear –   5

Using my rusty Dari on a man

Who sometime ago came here from Kabul.

Here I am with Warrington shopkeepers,

Edinburgh students, Woking mosque-goers.

Here I am, alone, in Costa Coffee,   10

With a lemon muffin and a flat white,

Like an online dater who's been stood up.

The Twitter commentariat love me,

But I heed the words and wisdom of Swift:

'It is the folly of too many to   15

Mistake the echo of a London

Coffee-house for the voice of the kingdom.'
Jonathan Swift, of course, not Taylor Swift;
She too makes political apercus.
Nightmares dress'd like daydreams; All you need'd   20
To do was stay; and a choice of endings.
Burning flames or paradise. Brexit, all.
Oh! Did I mention? I once took opium
'Twas at a wedding party in Iran.

Enter GOVE.

GOVE   Opium? Thou wants to be Coleridge?   25
            I took cocaine back in the day, you know.
            I was mad for it, totally mental.
            Colombian marching powder, Charlie,
            Beak, gak, blow: you name it, I snort'd it.

Enter LEADSOM.

LEADSOM   Ha! Amateurs, the both of you. Hardcore?   30
            I smok'd so much dope that they did call me
            The Ganja Queen, Miss Roberta Marley.

Enter RAAB.

RAAB   I too did partake of the sacred bud.
            But my tokes were most few and far between.

Enter HUNT.

HUNT   A cannabis lassi in India,   35

              That was my misdemeanour. Very slight.

              'Tis sure the narcotic equivalent

              Of running through fields of wheat as a child.

              Enter JOHNSON.

JOHNSON   I may have tak'n cocaine, but I say:

              Effect had it none. For all I know,   40

              It may well have been some icing sugar.

              I could perchance have bak'd a cake with it.

              As you all know, my policy on cake

              Is pro-having it and pro-eating it.

                                                 [Exeunt.

              Enter KUENSSBERG *with a cameraman.*

KUENSSBERG   What next, pray? The Saj: more horse than Aintree? 45

              Esther McVey: they call'd me Krystle Meth?

              Hancock, sweat-drench'd MDMA fucklord?

              This is absurd, ladies and gentlemen.

              Let's all get back to the matter in hand.

              To the vote! The first ballot of MPs   50

              Saw three candidates eliminat'd.

              [*Aside:*] Not lit'rally: 'tis not *The Hunger Games.*

              Leadsom, Harper, McVey, gone with the wind.

              Boris way out in front, follow'd by Hunt.

              Next day, Hancock withdrew. Now there were six.   55

              A TV debate, live on Channel 4.

Nay! Said Boris. I will not be present.

Washing his hair, or similar excuse.

[*Aside:*] 'Twas Father's Day: perchance tricky for him.

These the careful tactics of Team Boris;   60

Keep him out of sight as much as they could.

Heavily muzzl'd so he could not gaffe.

Public statements? Keep 'em vague, keep 'em short.

Piffle, poffle, wiffle, waffle. Crikey!

Schmoozing MPs in private, seeking votes.   65

'Twas a veritable charm offensive,

His backers ensur'd that 'twas long on charm

And short on offensiveness. No repeats

Of 'bum boys', 'picaninnies', 'letterbox'

Or anything to get him in hot water.   70

T'other thing Boris sought to avoid –

– And this went for every candidate –

– Was any endorsement from Chris Grayling.

Failing Grayling, the worst minister ever.

Who licens'd a ferry firm sans ferries.   75

'Grayling's backing Boris' came it anyway.

A communal, heartfelt sigh of relief

From all the other men left in the race.

They knew they had for sure dodg'd a bullet,

Just like Keanu Reeves in *The Matrix*.   80

> *[Exit Kuenssberg.*

SCENE 3

The Channel 4 studio.

Enter GOVE, HUNT, JAVID, RAAB *and* STEWART,
who each stand at a lit-up lectern. BORIS JOHNSON's *is empty.*

Enter newsreader KRISHNAN GURU-MURTHY, *who is moderating.*

GURU-MURTHY Welcome to the first leadership debate.
As you can see, we've nick'd the studio
Off *The Weakest Link*. Who will choose to bank?
And who, after tonight, will find that the
Conservative MPs say to them next: 5
'Thou art the weakest link. Goodbye.' Who knows?
As thou canst also see, one man's not here.
Though the empty lectern may well prove to
Answer any questions more honestly
Than the man who would be standing at it.   10

GOVE   I haven't taken coke for twenty years;
But looking at me tonight thou couldst be
Forgiven for thinking: 'Twenty minutes.'
My eyes are wild and I'm shouty crackers.
Wir'd, that's me, and not just for sound in here.   15
I've put everything on the line for this.
No, not that kind of line. Behave thyselves!

HUNT   I'm an entrepreneur. Observe this badge:

                The Union Jack upon my lapel.

                Patriotic, I thought it would appear,   20

                But actually under studio lights

                It looks more like something that a BA

                Steward would wear during a long-haul flight.

                Chicken or fish? Chicken or fish? Vegan?

                I'll just check with my colleague. Bear with me.   25

JAVID   I get things done. Lots of things. Many things.

                And I went to a comprehensive school

                Unlike all of thee. Charterhouse, Eton,

                Dr. Challoner's and Robert Gordon.

RAAB   I'm a karate man. Anyone here   30

                Seen *Trading Places*? Eddie Murphy says:

                'I'm a karate man. Karate men

                Bruise on the inside. Don't show our weakness.'

                That's me. Bruise on the inside for Brexit.

                I won't rule out suspending Parliament.   35

                The minute we signal to the EU

                That we're willing to stay post-Hallowe'en,

                That's when we lose our best shot at a deal.

JAVID   Thou canst not deliver democracy

                By trashing democracy. 'Tis absurd.   40

                We're trying to choose a Prime Minister;

                Thou wouldst style thyself strongman, dictator.

HUNT   The Saj doth speak the truth on this issue.

              This scheme is not what Parliament stands for,

              And the people would never accept it.   45

STEWART   I'm the only one here who can bear to

              Admit weakness, uncertainty, or doubt.

              Machismo is itself no strategy.

              Thou art all trying to be the toughest.

              I am trying to be realistic,   50

              And so I am accus'd of defeatism.

              All these no-deal emperors have no clothes.

              They are all proud, revengeful, ambitious;

              With more offences at my beck than they

              Have thoughts to put them in, imagination to   55

              Give them shape, or time to act them in. What

              Should such fellows as they do crawling

              Between earth and heaven? They are arrant knaves, all.

              Believe none of them. Wait only until

              They sheathe their swords for lack of argument.   60

              'Tis like trying to cram a whole series

              Of rubbish bags into the rubbish bin.

              'Thou canst do it! Just believe in the bin!

              Believe in Britain!' 'Tis arrant nonsense.

              I must also discuss tariff schedules.   65

              I'm fun at parties, as you can imagine.

              Thee, the audience, clearly love me.

              And most of the country would vote for me

              Over everyone else here (or not here.)

              But we all know our electorate now;   70

Old, white, male, and not watching Channel 4.

HUNT   If Team Boris won't allow him out to
              Debate with five pretty friendly colleagues,
              How will he cope with EU governments?

GURU-MURTHY What thou say makes sense, of course, but know this. 75
              We have already gone far beyond sense.
              This is like a passage out of Kafka,
              Or down the rabbit hole in Wonderland.
              Politics: show business for the ugly.
              'Tis like *Love Island* without the six-packs.   80

GOVE   One could perchance title it 'Gove Island'.

GURU-MURTHY 'Tis the best line of the evening.

GOVE   Thank you.

*The lights go down. When they go up again a few moments
later, the lecterns have been replac'd by stools, RAAB has been
replac'd by JOHNSON, and GURU-MURTHY has been
replac'd by newsreader EMILY MAITLIS.*

MAITLIS   Now for the BBC, and with Boris.
              Observe the five men perch'd upon their stools.   85
              'Tis not the world's worst Boyzone tribute band,
              Though thou wouldst be forgiv'n for thinking so.
              'Tis possible, too, for Mr Johnson,

That Boyzone are helping run his campaign.

He says it best when he says nothing at all.   90

[*Aside:*] Well, maybe just Ronan Keating.

HUNT   I'm an—

ALL (TOGETHER) Entrepreneur. Yes, we know that.

GOVE   I was first here to advocate Brexit.

              I start'd this, so I will finish it.   95

MAITLIS   Sorry, Michael. That line's from *Mastermind*.

GOVE   From *The Weakest Link* to *Mastermind*, with

              A bit of *The Apprentice* thrown in too.

JAVID   I will give 110 per cent.

JOHNSON   I'll mention my Muslim great-grandfather   100

              But when Abdullah the imam phones in

              I'll call him 'our friend'. Forgotten his name?

              Perish the thought! I always speak with care.

              Just ask Nazanin Zaghari-Ratcliffe.

STEWART   I will take off my tie two questions in,   105

              To get back to a bit of reality.

              Just saying that, it makes no sense at all.

MAITLIS   Tonight's not just about Brexit, of course.

Questions on tax cuts, public services,

Islamophobia and climate change.   110

Anyone going to give a straight answer?

All five candidates are silent.

MAITLIS   Not to any question? Not even one?

Still they are silent.

MAITLIS   Now back to you in the studio, Huw.

[Exit Maitlis.

Enter KUENSSBERG.

KUENSSBERG   That's my line. Not to mention the fact that

Thou art in the studio already, no?   115

On the voting went. Stewart next to go.

The light on STEWART *goes out.*

[Exit Stewart.

KUENSSBERG   Then the Saj.

The light on JAVID *goes out too.*

[Exit Javid.

KUENSSBERG   And then Gove, by just two votes.

Some controversy here. Gove supporters

Accus'd the stout yeomen in Team Boris   120
Of having lent some votes to Jeremy Hunt.
The memories of Iago burn'd strong;
Referendum psychodrama, rerun.
Perchance they thought Hunt would be easier
To beat. 'Theresa in trousers,' they said.   125
'Twas impossible to prove either way.

The light on GOVE *goes out too.*

So now there were two. But afore they go
Head to head, a brief interlude for thee,
Brought by the Metropolitan Police.

[Exeunt.

SCENE 4

A flat in Camberwell.

Enter JOHNSON *and his girlfriend,* CARRIE SYMONDS.

Before either can say anything, there's a knock on the door.
SYMONDS, *who's nearer, opens it. Enter two police officers,*
TROILUS *and* CRESSIDA.

TROILUS   I am Detective Constable Troilus.

CRESSIDA   I'm Detective Constable Cressida.

TROILUS   Evening, all.

CRESSIDA   We do still say that, thou knowest.

JOHNSON   How can we help thee, good men of the law?   5

SYMONDS   One of them's a woman. 'Tis unlike thee
            Not to notice a small detail like that.

CRESSIDA   We have heard reports of a disturbance.

JOHNSON   A disturbance? Where?

CRESSIDA   Here.   10

JOHNSON   There on the stair?

CRESSIDA   No. Here. In this room. Thine neighbours did call.

            TROILUS *consults his notes.*

TROILUS   They said they heard thee, Ms Carrie Symonds,
            Shouting, 'Get off me!'

JOHNSON   The 'with' is missing.   15
            'Get off WITH me.' A phrase I am fond of.

CRESSIDA   'Tis no laughing matter, sir.

JOHNSON   Aye. Sorry.

TROILUS   Also, that you, Ms Symonds, said loudly:
               'Thou hast spill'd wine on my sofa, thou clot.   20
               Thou cares for nothing as thou art spoil'd.'

JOHNSON   'Tis true. The wine part, at least. Problem is
               The wine was cheap – Portuguese paint stripper,
               Special offer at Waitrose, don't you know? –
               And the sofa expensive. Wrong way round.   25
               Had it been up to me, I'd have gone for
               A bottle of Châteauneuf-du-Pape, aye,
               And a sofa from *World of Interiors*.

TROILUS   Thou art saying this is just etiquette?

JOHNSON   Basically, aye.   30

CRESSIDA   What about the laptop?

JOHNSON   What about it?

CRESSIDA   'Leave my laptop alone.'
               That's also what the neighbours said you said.

JOHNSON   A chap's browser history is a matter   35
               For him and him alone, wouldn't you say?

               TROILUS *and* CRESSIDA *confer.*

TROILUS   Nothing to see here. Thank you for your time.

                                                    [Exeunt.

SCENE 5

Enter KUENSSBERG *with a cameraman*

KUENSSBERG The story damag'd Boris, but not much;
            Not, for sure, amongst the party faithful,
            Who came to hustings up and down the land.
            To Birmingham and Bournemouth, Exeter,
            Carlisle, Manchester, Belfast and York,   5
            To Darlington, Perth, Nottingham, Cardiff,
            To Maidstone, Cheltenham and Wyboston,
            Colchester and Canning Town: 16 sites.

                                          [Exit Kuenssberg.

Enter JOHNSON *and* HUNT.

JOHNSON   To the doom-and-gloom merchants, I say this:
            On November the First, deal or no deal   10
            [*Aside:*] And not the Noel Edmonds programme,
            There will be clean drinking water, planes will fly,
            There will be milk solids, and glucose too,
            And whey for the Mars Bars. Because, you know,
            Where there's a will, there's a whey, as I say.   15

HUNT   'Tis stirring stuff, Boris, and I don't mean
            The great mixing vats in the Mars factory.

But belief alone won't and can't cut it.

Rhetoric is not enough. We need more;

Hard graft, focus, attention to detail.   20

That means ev'ry eventuality,

Ev'ry law or statutory instrument,

Ev'ry industry. And every part of Britain.

We cannot leave on a wing and a prayer.

I offer thee my special ten-point plan.   25

One. An immediate escalation

Of No Deal preparations. All August

Leave for civil servants will be cancell'd.

No holiday villas, no beach hotels.

In Provence, Gascony and the Dordogne;   30

In Tuscany, Umbria and Venice,

My name will be mud, or something ruder.

Jeremy Rhyming Slang, they will call me.

Two. Make a 'No Deal' Cabinet Task Force.

Like *DIY SOS*, but without   35

Nick Knowles, or an uplifting backstory.

Three. Convene a negotiating team

From all corners of the Tory Party.

Four. Engage with European leaders

Over the summer. Pref'rably in the   40

Villas the civil servants can't now use.

Five. A National Logistics Committee

To keep goods coming in and out of Britain

If No Deal comes to pass. Don't tell Grayling.

Six. A No Deal Budget for September.   45

Seven. A No Deal Relief Programme, for

Fishing and farming sectors who need help.
Eight. Tariffs. Blah blah. Still working on this.
Nine. Customs solutions. See point above.
Ten. Decide with one month to go whether   50
We can get a deal through in time or not.
There thou goest, Boris. Ten more points than yours.

JOHNSON   Eh? Come again? I didn't quite catch that.

HUNT   Wast thou not listening?

JOHNSON   My friend, I confess,   55
           My attention had wander'd for a mo.
           I was painting a bus.

HUNT   Were doing what?

JOHNSON   I get old wooden crates and I paint them.
           I like to paint buses. I make models   60
           Of them, and put happy passengers in.

HUNT   Dost thou write on the side of them, perchance?
           Three hundred and fifty million pounds?

JOHNSON   Let's have less of this talking Britain down!

HUNT   I ask thee this. If, as Prime Minister,   65
           When Hallowe'en comes around, full of
           Spooks and ghouls and freaks and fools—

JOHNSON   *Rentaghost*!

HUNT   —thou hast still not deliver'd Brexit, will
            thou then resign?   70

JOHNSON   Stop talking Britain down!

HUNT   'Tis not an answer.
            Thou hast said: 'the 31st, do or die.'
            If thou will not for sure fall on thy sword,
            'Tis not do or die. All that matters then   75
            Is that thou dost remain in Number Ten.
            'Twill be your biggest Remain commitment.
            As Mrs Thatcher was not for turning,
            So thou also will be not for Leaving.

JOHNSON   We must all believe.   80

HUNT   'Tis still not an answer.

JOHNSON   Get off the hamster wheel of doom.

HUNT   Again.

JOHNSON   Optimism!

HUNT   'Tis like waiting for Godot. Or BoJo.   85
            Shame most of the votes are already in.

JOHNSON   Of course. I wouldn't have agreed to this
            If it would make the slightest diff'rence.
            Though I greatly admire thine ability
            To change thine mind. Once Remain, now Leave, no?   90

HUNT   And in turn I admire your ability
            Never to provide one small, straight answer.

                                                        [Exeunt.

SCENE 6

Queen Elizabeth Hall, London.

A large AUDIENCE *gather in front of a stage.*

Enter KUENSSBERG *with a cameraman.*

KUENSSBERG At last, the moment has come. 'Tis now time
            For the leadership results to be call'd.
            I'll spare thee the tedious preamble:
            Party bigwigs thanking all and sundry,
            Spinning suspense out as much as they can.   5
            Get on with it! 'Tis not *The X Factor*,
            Nor *Strictly Come Dancing*, nor *Big Brother*.
            To no one's surprise, the winner? Boris.
            By the decent margin of two to one.

                                                    [Exit Kuenssberg.

Enter JOHNSON, *who gets up on the stage.*

JOHNSON   I begin by thanking my opponent;   10
                 A font of excellent ideas, all of
                 Which I intend to steal forthwith. I jest?
                 Not at all. I am *la gazza ladra*,
                 The thieving magpie. (Not Gazza himself.)
                 But back to Jeremy for just a sec.   15
                 A formidable campaigner indeed,
                 And a great politician. Nice words, eh?
                 An emollient for when I sack him.
                 Next, I would like to thank Theresa May.
                 For years I agitat'd agin her,   20
                 But now's the time to be magnanimous.
                 There will be many who question all this;
                 The prudence of a BoJo leadership.
                 No one has a monopoly on wisdom.
                 But 'tis we Tories with the best insights   25
                 Into how to manage the jostling sets
                 Of instincts in the human heart. (Nice line.)
                 The instincts to own thine own house, to earn
                 And spend thine own money, look
                 After thine own family. Good instincts,   30
                 Proper instincts, noble instincts, them all.
                 I read in my *Financial Times* today,
                 Devot'd reader that I am, that no
                 Incoming leader has ever fac'd
                 Such a daunting set of circumstances.   35
                 I look at thee and think: 'dost thou look daunt'd?'

JOHNSON *pauses. There is silence.*

JOHNSON   I say again: dost thou look daunt'd?

AUDIENCE   [*Quiet*] No.

JOHNSON   I was expecting a bit more, thou knowest.
            Thee don't look remotely daunt'd to me.   40
            Nor remotely sentient, some of you.
            Remember our mantra, chant it daily.
            Deliver Brexit, unite the country,
            And defeat Jeremy Corbyn. All those.
            Together they spell out D-U-D. Dud.   45
            Ah, 'tis not such a good acronym, that.
            But, my friends, we forgot the final 'E'.
            [*Aside:*] Not that kind of E, Govey. Settle down.
            'E' for 'energise'. And that spells out 'dude'.
            Dude, we're going to energise Britain.   50
            [*Aside:*] A sequel to the film *Dude, Where's My Car?*
            We will once again believe in ourselves.
            Like some slumbering giant, we're going
            To rise and ping off the guy ropes of
            Self-doubt and negativity, we are.   55
            The doubters, the doomsters, the gloomsters: they
            Are all going to get it wrong again.
            Those who bet agin us will lose their shirts.
            Triumph or failure, twin impostors, are
            My personal responsibility.   60
            So never mind the backstop. The buck stops here.
                                                      [*Exeunt.*

SCENE 7

Outside Number 10 Downing Street.

Enter KUENSSBERG *with a cameraman, and* JOHNSON.

KUENSSBERG   We end as we began. All life's a stage.

He has his exits and his entrances;

And this man in his time plays many parts,

His acts being seven ages. At first the schoolboy,

Deaf till eight with 'glue ear', a subdu'd child;   5

Then competitive, determin'd to win

No matter the nature of the contest.

Captain of the School at Eton College.

And then the Oxford student; a scholar

Of the classics, Latin and Ancient Greek.   10

President of the Oxford Union,

Hearty stalwart of the Bullingdon Club.

And then the correspondent in Brussels;

Sexing up endless boring EU tales.

They're intending to ban prawn-flavour'd crisps!   15

They want to straighten out our bananas!

They make condoms too small for Englishmen!

All these, only the barest grain of truth.

Fourth, the star TV personality,

Bumbling and blust'ring, waffling and wheezing.   20

Have I Got News For You made him famous;

The Tory who reach'd parts others could not.

And so to number five, Mayor of London;

Boris bikes, zip wires and garden bridges.

A launch pad for national ambition.   25

And so he play'd his part. The sixth age shifts

Into the aspiring would-be statesman;

Leave campaigner par excellence, Foreign

Secretary *sans pareil* in every way.

[*Aside:*] Take that as you like: 'tis no compliment.   30

Now, seventh, and last, but by no means least,

The job at which he's always tipp'd his hat.

Prime Minister, *primus inter pares*,

First Lord of the Treasury and all that.

Into a situation still fluid,   35

With no one knowing how Brexit will end.

How'll he fare? Let's ask the man himself.

JOHNSON   What now for me? Have I not ever said

How that ambitious Boris would not cease

Till he'd kindl'd the United Kingdom   40

Upon the right and party of himself?

Over the years I have denounc'd the hope

Of this ever coming to pass. More chance,

Said I, of being reincarnat'd

As an olive, lock'd in a fridge, finding   45

Elvis still alive on Mars, or being

Decapitat'd by flying Frisbee.

Playing to the gallery, all of those,

As well you have guess'd. 'Tis mine now, at last.

Is my struggle now end'd? Have my rivals   50

All melt'd into air, into thin air:

And, like the baseless fabric of my vision,

The cloud-capp'd towers, the gorgeous palaces,

The solemn temples, the great globe itself,

Yea, all which it inherit, shall dissolve   55

And, like this insubstantial pageant fad'd,

Leave not a rack behind? Who now can tell?

Indeed, it is a strange dispos'd time:

So without ado let's to it pell-mell

If not to heaven, then hand in hand to hell!   60

                         [Exeunt omnes.

END.

Acknowledgements

Thanks to Joel Simons and Madiya Altaf at Blink for their
commitment to this project, and to the politicians of the
United Kingdom for their commitment to satire.